20/20

Wisdom

20/20 Wisdom

A COLLECTION OF EXPRESSIONS AND REFLECTIONS
FROM AN EXTRAORDINARY YEAR

COMPILED BY

JIM SECORD

ISBN: 978-1-68201-135-5

Format and Cover Design by Liz Dwyer of North Star Press.
Printed in the United States of America.

P★ Polaris Publications
an imprint of
North Star Press of Saint Cloud Inc.
w w w . n o r t h s t a r p r e s s . c o m

Dedication

For the 615,596* Americans who gave up their lives to the Pandemic, and for their families and friends who still mourn them.

May they be at peace.

*As of June 14, 2021

Introduction

We're all in this together

What do we remember about 2020? Ask fifty people, and you'll most likely receive fify different responses.

Take for example, December 16, 2020, when 3,448 Americans died during the Covid-19 pandemic. I recall it being reported that more were lost that day than during 9/11, or Pearl Harbor, or any other catastrophic day in the history of our country. That had a huge impact on me, while to others, it would be something else.

In many cases, friends, relatives, and those questioned in the news, will say they became vulnerable, frightened, lonely, or angry. They were often in a state of psychological vertigo, a dizzying sensation of whirling and loss of equilibrium. Then there were those who said that 2020 was a year of reflection, "of getting things done," of rediscovery and of finding new "purpose" in their lives. And of course, it was said to be a virtual reconnecting with old friends and distant family members.

But it wasn't only the pandemic that captured our lives. We dealt with one of the most contentious national elections since our democracy was founded, witnessed millions of job losses, faced unbridled racism, rebellion, economic inequality, and political divisiveness.

Without question, 2020 was a year that will be in people's memories for decades to come, because most all of us have a story to tell. Some more dramatic and painful to be sure. Just as you, the readers of this book can recite your experiences, those who specifically wrote for this book, have recited their own personal impressions, expressions, reflections, and wisdom. It is to these dear friends and family members, that I address the next portion of this Introduction.

****

Some of you, upon receiving the invitation to participate in this project, got back to me with questions that went something like these: Why are you (Jim) doing this? Why are you taking this on? What do you hope to accomplish? One of you even wrote: "You must be a masochist to go through this again" (to which he added..."but we're thrilled you're doing it")

I didn't have a complete answer. Was it because of the success of my previous book, *Vintage Wisdom*? Or, was it because I truly wanted to hear how you were dealing with one of the most challenging times of your lives?

It wasn't until I read the introduction to the *Book of Ecclesiastes (New American Bible)* that I found a possible explanation to my question. It reads: "Its author Qoheleth is actually a title, and it perhaps means 'assembler'...or 'collector' of wisdom sayings. ...The book comprises an extended reflective essay employing autobiographical narrative, proverbs, parables and allegories."

Bingo! My light went on. Behind my desire to collect meaningful stories, it was to "assemble", for future generations, what happened in your minds and hearts during this time of fear, separation, loneliness, political and social unrest, enormous sickness, and loss of life. And also, for most of you, a time to reconnect with family, albeit in a less accustomed way.

On a narrative level, my desire was to also create a collection of mini-stories that can be pulled off a bookshelf (or out of a box) twenty-five, fifty, or even a hundred years from now—a capsule of what this generation, from young to almost ancient—were thinking during this very distinct year.

If nothing else were to be said in this Introduction, it would be sufficient to state that the common denominator of your writings is our need for one another, our families, our friends, our faith communities, and all those people we care for, and who care for us. We are, indeed, social beings, driven to be dependent on each other.

****

About the contents of this book:

You, my family and friends, far exceeded my expectations with your responses! While I believed that a hundred entries would produce a meaningful document, I hoped, best case, to receive 125 contributions. In actuality, you'll find 164 entries from 192 individuals. This allows for the twenty-eight couples that chose to write your stories together.

It was purposeful that I wanted to include several decades and genders of lives within these pages. As a result:

* 7 of you are from ages 0 to 20
* 10 from ages 21 to 40
* 39 from ages 41 to 60
* 107 from ages 61 to 80
* 29 over the age of 81

In terms of gender, 84 of you are female and 108 male.

Although geographically, the vast majority of inclusions are from Americans (United States), friends living in Canada, Wales, Russia, and China are included in this book.

If there was a challenge in editing 20/20 Wisdom, it was with regard to length. The limit in words was to be 250. With "help", most of you kept within this boundary. I know this was difficult for some of you, and I appreciate the efforts you made, through your own redrafts. In the cases where the guideline wasn't possible to meet, I attempted to keep the spirit of your writings intact. The same would be true for other minor editing. If in any way, your contribution was altered to your disappointment, please accept my sincere apology.

As outlined in my original request letter, I have disguised the respondents' full names, positions, organizations or titles. All are arranged alphabetically by first name and birth year, of which there was a separation of ninety-six years between the youngest (as written by their father) and the oldest participant. Hooray for longevity!

*****

Today, we have only started the conversation as to who we are, and how we are to move forward. We want something to come out of all the chaos from this past year; the pain, the frustration, the losses, the anger. However, many of us don't know what that is.

We itch all over and scratch our minds to discover what we need to hold on to, and what to discard.

At the beginning of my eighty-fifth year, I've come to believe that I have little or no control of anything, outside of what I do personally. Upon reflection, I am attempting to release myself from the duality that has driven me during this time of the pandemic... fear, worry, judging, fatigue... and back to my faith-centered belief that as long as I'm alive, there's work to be done; whatever that may be.

Part of this resolve, along with wishing it for others, is to understand that to be human is to be vulnerable. We are easily bruised, and of feeling not up to the task of getting ourselves back to the "new normal". The positive mental hitchhikers we pick up along this road could be: listening to those with whom we philosophically or politically have differences; empathy and engagement with communities we have kept at a distance; discarding the biases and prejudices we learned from our childhood (and continued to keep); and of relying on one-dimensional informational resources (which traps us into imitating "one-way-isms").

We live in a time of immense ambiguity. Putting aside the pundits, no one actually knows what the next four (or forty) years will bring, even when fifty are questioned, we may receive fifty responses. As the fifty-first, my personal belief is that we must rebuild a foundation of trust, and if we're to pull through the reckoning of the past sixteen months, regardless of how the American democratic pendulum swings, we have the responsibility ...all of us... to bring our country together.

As the great Sufi mystic Hafiz wrote:

"NOTHING IS EVER OUT OF REACH".

It is time to re-set. Time to move on. Time to look at 2020 as a metaphor on life, an awakening of who we are, of the desire to become the best that can be, to get away from hate, from the remnants of "bad history", from distrust, from what holds us back from caring for each other.

As noted in the cut line below the word Introduction, "We are all in this together", and to remember that

God Loves Us All.

Gratefully,

Jim Secord, 1936

jimsecord36@gmail.com

The Invitation

Dear Family and Friends,

The last time I wrote a letter like this was in 2018... at the age of 82... when I was feeling called to reconnect with cherished friends from over the years. At that time, I was curious about how they would respond to a request to share one piece of their personal wisdom with others.

To my amazement, 95% responded and that effort culminated into the book *Vintage Wisdom*, which is now in its 2nd printing.

Vintage Wisdom was to be the one and only book in my lifetime, until 2020 happened. A year like none other! Once again, I find myself reflecting on wisdom, your wisdom... about how this year has impacted your life.

So I ask:

What has the pandemic and 2020 done to and for you?

Has it been a time of reflection, hope, of some despair... and maybe, even a reawakening of both your heart and your soul?

Within the framework of Vintage Wisdom, my hope is that you will lend your thoughts—your WISDOM—about how COVID-19 and other significant events in 2020 have changed your life. While I hope you will dive deep into yourself, with the understanding it may be a bit challenging, please don't let this exercise overwhelm you. It is, above all, about how YOU are dealing with one of the most unusual times in your life.

Should you decide to participate (which I earnestly hope you will), here are some thoughts to consider when penning your response:

- Has the pandemic and other dramatic events strengthened relationships with your family, community and/or faith... or fostered greater personal isolation, or both?
- Have you found yourself grieving losses in your life during this time? If so, what have you noticed?
- How have your priorities been realigned during this time of uncertainty?
- What are the most significant blessings or gifts for you that have come out of the pandemic?

With your responses I'm once again looking to produce a book that will include your Wisdom...whether it be a paragraph, a quote, or something longer (limited to a maximum of 250 words, please).

As you write your response, you may want to do this in partnership with another (husband/wife/partner)—writing individually or together. Each written contribution will be attributed to your first name (or should there be a doubling up of names, your last name initial will be included). And since I'm anticipating at least a few generations of responses, please include your year of birth. For example, mine will be "Jim '36".

You will each receive a copy of this latest book of wisdom, once it is published in 2021; perhaps to be kept by your family for years to come.

I'm very excited at the prospect of you being part of this project. And thankful for your consideration in participating. With that in mind, may I have your reply by January 1st?

With enormous gratitude,

Jim Secord
jimsecord36@gmail.com

I believe it will take years to fully process the life lessons that this pandemic held. What I do know is that we all found a strength in us that we may not have known existed. Through incredible loss, painful separations, and hopes dashed, we found the fortitude to pick ourselves up again, and again... AND AGAIN. We lent our strength to friends, family, loved ones, and strangers, and we borrowed strength from others when we needed a hand getting back up ourselves. There is tremendous beauty in our collective resiliency and compassion.

-Alecia S. 1981

1

During the pandemic, I watched loss,

I watched growth,

I watched boundaries get moved across.

Many gave an oath

to finally care for their peers,

give others their trust,

move past their fears.

And of course, I was no exception.

But I didn't go through the loss, or the pain-

but from the inception,

my way of life had been maintained.

Many weren't as lucky as I ended up being,

and for the first time, I felt like I was truly seeing.

Watching my peers,

seeing their fear,

I can finally truly understand

how lucky I really, really am.

-Alex S. 2005

In the Jewish tradition, the ritual of Havdalah on Saturday evenings separates the holiness of Shabbat from the "ordinary" week, with prayers for hope and peace in the week to come. This pandemic has been a significant separation from our "ordinary" lives and has reshaped our experiences as individuals, families and communities. The pandemic has created overwhelming loss of human life, and deep uncertainty, and economic instability for millions, even billions, around the world. Yet there is renewed hope that with this unintended pause we can mindfully and empathically rebuild the future in a way that mirrors the prayers of Havdalah.

"Havdalah means: separate yourself from fraud and exploitation; be fair and honest with all people.

Havdalah means: separate yourself from indifference to the poor and the deprived, the sick and the aged; work to ease their despair and their loneliness.

Havdalah means: separate yourself from hatred and violence; promote peace among people and nations···

Open up for us, Adonai our God, this week, and every week, gates of light and gates of blessing so that all who enter may know peace and goodness."

~Mishkan T'filah, A Reform Siddur, p. 6

-Alison S. 1983

Never have I felt more alone, and yet more connected to the world.

My partner had left to work out of state just before the pandemic and has continued to be there for the last 10 months. So, alone I have quarantined and worried about my loved ones and the world. Watching in horror the number of people dying. Feeling warmth as I saw people supporting each other in ways I never thought possible. Constant yo-yo of emotions. Immense gratitude and fear changing by the day, hour, minute. FaceTiming with my sisters brought tears and laughter. Some constant to look forward to. Virtual daily exercise with a couple of woman that have enriched my life more than I could have ever imagined. The personal growth and support that I've experienced knowing them has been a wonderful surprise. An unexpected visit from my son, time alone with deep conversations and fun. Always pulling my heart this way and that.

There was a fire at my condo, yet it was barely a blip on my radar. 2020 has been a huge reminder of what truly is important. What and who makes our heart sing? How short our lives are here on earth. What mark do we want to leave? What do we want to fill our minds and days with? 2020 made me more mindful, more connected to those I love and those I didn't even know I needed.

-Angela M. 1969

The Wisdom of an Unhurried Life

The cacophony of life was subdued by force in 2020 through lockdowns and social distance. Though despair sometimes cast its shadow, this season of my life has taught me the blessings of being unhurried.

An unhurried heart nurtures deeper relationship, even if connected with loved ones through a screen.

An unhurried body experiences deeper rest and reflection. God's voice is more easily heard and received in quiet stillness.

An unhurried soul fosters deeper faith through meditation and prayer. Worshipping God's sovereignty, power and majesty refreshes a weary spirit.

An unhurried mind rejoices in learning. Shuttered busyness affords time and space for growth.

An unhurried life acknowledges and receives blessings. Contentment and peace flourish in the rich soil of a grateful heart.

May these discoveries be cherished through the rest of my life.

-Anne D. 1959

*T*he COVID shutdown for me, along with my growing older and not being able to do everything like I used to do, has

brought me to my knees.

I'm taking things harder, it seems, after all the chaos, disaster, elections, and the downing of some of my favorite philanthropic programs that I was very active in.

A lot of what has been reported in the world has also taken the starch out of me. I'm even more convinced that I don't have as much patience, when I can't find "goodness" with more of the doings that are happening all around me.

My Faith has become my safe haven more than ever before.

-Babs K. 1930

Devastating pandemic
Cruel isolation
Yet, life finds a way.

-Barry H. 1942

"Nearer my God to Thee"

covers how the COVID-19 pandemic has affected me.

I cannot remember a time in my life when I did not believe and feel the presence of God. However, during these troubled days I am so much more aware. I believe God has a plan, but at the same time, I believe that we mortals can mess it up. I am not with the group who are blissfully going their own ways, because, "if it is my time, so be it". I am exercising care, truly amazed at the resiliency we have and creativity learning to cope in so many new ways, as we worship on Facebook, with the familiar setting of the same sanctuary and same faith leaders, participating in virtual communion; we attend the same committee meetings, do Bible study, prepare for necessary appointments; all on Zoom. We even celebrate family gatherings on Zoom. Not bad for those of us well into our 80s!

As my life continues at a fairly comfortable level, I'm mindful of the struggles younger people have managing children with distance learning, and handling their employment requirements. And those who are delivering the services—the care givers, the educators and the leaders on local, state and national level. Their stresses are mind boggling and I strive to do my part by staying out of the way. My life is easy, I cannot and should not complain.

-Bea O. 1935

Like many, we have been in isolation since early March. But, every day brings something new to enjoy from our twenty-fifth floor view—a panorama of changing cloud formations, a different hue of light that plays on the downtown buildings, the redesigned park that emerged last summer across the street.

We are thankful for each other, our family, and good friends. We are also thankful for small surprises—a call from a friend we knew long ago, a gift box of flaky, buttery croissants that take us back to our travels in France, an offer by a young man in our building to run errands for us.

Except for our daily walks, we don't go "out" so we go "inward". We spend more time thinking about what is most important to us. We read voraciously to understand better what is happening in our world and in our community.

We grieve deeply about the pain caused by COVID, the divisiveness in our nation, and the vast inequities in our society; but we get up each morning knowing that we must work toward what will make a better society. We are passionate about racial justice and are trying to live out the words of Cornell West, "Justice is what love looks like in public."

Life is a gift.
It is not to be squandered,
even in isolation.
So, let us be thankful.

-Bebe B. 1930 & Rollie B. 1929

"When we have shuffled off this mortal coil,
Must give us pause, there's the respect,
That makes calamity of so long life."
— Shakespeare

This year, defined by so many important events, has forced me to evaluate my perspective regarding my country, my community, and most immediately, myself. For quite some time I have been aware of my ever decreasing time until I "shuffle off this mortal coil", but 2020 has precipitated a new urgency. This past year, and honestly, the past several years, has warranted me to examine what our country and our community are, rather than accept my acquired perception of what is. I hope, as we go forward and "re-enter" this world, as the vaccine gives rise to increased movement and freedom, to examine each day before me, as it begins, and have the ability to pause and discern where my time and attention will be most meaningful, and to enter the day with renewed gratitude.

-Becky K. 1952

Racially and politically divided. Combative. Divisive. Broken dreams.

When asked by news outlets to capture the essence of 2020 in just a few words, those above were some of what readers identified.

The theme of division comes through loud and clear. It's hard to believe that we as a nation have ever been been more trapped by the beliefs that separate us from one another. One might hope beliefs could liberate us. Make us better neighbors. Make us better citizens. Perhaps we need to look elsewhere.

What if we were to focus less on beliefs—whose are right and whose are wrong—and instead, come from a place of covenant. As my good friend, the Rev. Victoria Safford, writes "Covenant is a promise I keep to myself, about the kind of person I want to be, the kind of life I mean to have, together with other people and all other living things."

It takes courage to live without
creed or credo—
no man-made walls to sleep within;
no roof to keep out the rain. But
such a roof can blind us to the stars.
Why not choose instead to live from
covenant, willing to listen to songs
sung in many voices. To recognize
the inadequacy of mere tolerance,
and replace it with authentic respect
and deep compassion.

-Bill M. 1948

As a person who has lived a primarily solitary lifestyle, I at first didn't believe I would have to make a major adjustment in my living practices and would only encounter minor adjustments. I was quite wrong, but not in a way I could have imagined.

An idea, a theory, began to develop and grow in me, and it has continued unabated since the pandemic began. While I worry on a regular basis for my sons in New York City, I began to realize that I was dealing with, of all things, optimism. This was greatly spurred by my re-reading of Thomas Paine's classic work of 1776, *Common Sense.* What struck me like a ton of bricks was its representation of what America could be then… and now. Paine wrote,

"We have it in our power to begin the world over again".

I agree with our founding fathers in my sense that this could/must be the onset of a new era, a reawakening of so many of the values that resulted in a Republic all those years ago. Facing political chaos and a raging virus, our democracy is holding for now. Our challenge is to find courage within ourselves to carve a new path toward an improved nation, to last and make progress for another two hundred years.

I've become accepting of our national trauma but I'm convinced there is a new day coming where we right ourselves and set off to lead the world again.

-*Bill S. 1937*

We have experienced great pain in 2020 from **fear**, ANGER, emotional exhaustion, death of friends, and *loss* of physical contact. All punctuated by the inability to give or receive hugs to bolster strength.

That said, we continue to appreciate the significance of friends by finding hope in unexpected places, focusing on the good in others, and understanding there are some days we think we know **a lot**—and other days we know nothing.

Coping has brought us joy where we least expect it, and within ourselves, deep reflection while realigning future priorities.

To embrace the present, we see twinkles in the eyes of others, but look forward to a day in the future when masks can be removed to unveil the smiles beneath.

-Bill V. 1954 & Sheri B. 1957

Many of us have experienced what can be referenced as a 20/20 situation—one where we find ourselves on the "outside looking in". These can happen in business settings, general family life, spousal interactions or even sudden/significant health issues. They are all forms of life altering events, some short term and some for the long haul. Regardless, they all blindside us when they occur, as did COVID-19 this year.

Were you caught in the web of one or more of these situations? I was, and the it forced me to stay close to home, and curtail my interaction with friends, and on and on. There has been, however, a huge plus as I have much more time to listen and address the cares and concerns of family members, my doctors, and my God.

Most enriching for me is when I take the time to turn off the TV, the radio, set down the book, the wrench, or whatever, and simply let my inner thoughts meander where they take me. Oh the thoughts—sadness, joy, inner peace beyond description. I also look outdoors and see the birds adapting to their environment daily. So, too, can we adapt!

2020 is a golden opportunity for all of us to get a better 20/20 look at our lives. Proverbs 1:33 speaks volumes:

"'Whoever listens to me will live in safety and at peace without fear of harm"

-Bill W. 1936

Throughout 2020, I was continuously reminded of the classic Native American parable "The Tale of Two Wolves." Within each of us exists the battle between two wolves—one good, and one evil—*and the one we feed is the one who wins.*

This has been a year like no other, filled with often unbelievable and immeasurable blessings, lessons, and challenges.

2020 was the brightest year. Topping our list of blessings was the arrival of our twin daughters on Easter Vigil. Working from home, and the complete inability to travel, helped ensure I was ever-present in our children's new and exciting lives. The plethora of simple experiences also contributed to a year of joy and togetherness. Frequent walks in the neighborhood, long drives on rainy and cold days, home cooking on a scale never before realized, working in the garden, near daily "movie nights"—all, while feeling incredibly lucky we had each other to witness and share every day together. And, there were also new, deepened, and revitalized friendships that were each God-given.

2020 WAS THE DARKEST YEAR. And, while we were able to escape much of what infected our society this year, we still bore witness to immense pain. Isolation. Loneliness. Fear. Panic. Injustice. Racism. Carelessness. Selfishness. Division. Violence. Insanity. Rage. Struggle. Lies. Fires. Loss. Closures. Unemployment. Lockdown. Death.

I have tremendous faith and hope for the future.

-Billy S. 1976

The pandemic has been a blessing and a scourge. The main blessing is the renewed relationship with my two daughters; especially my middle daughter who disowned me and my wife about 4 years ago. It came back as quickly as it had disappeared in late summer of this year.

My understanding of perseverance in difficulties has been strengthened. My 3rd grade teacher taught me a word that has become my word for 2020. The word is: **STICKTOITTIVENESS**. Never stop praying and believing and clinging to the blessings and the benefits of what you are learning as you are being dragged, naked, through the broken glass of your experience. Here is a quote that states the way I feel:

"The rewards for those who persevere far exceed the pain that must precede the victory."
-Ted Engstrom.

I never gave up on my daughter and the reward has been glorious.

This year I have experienced the loss of friends and mentors but in that sadness I have clung, more fiercely, to the things I had learned and experienced from them.

-Bob F. 1948

I celebrated 40 years of marriage in the summer of 2020 and because of the COVID-19 pandemic, it became my most memorable anniversary. I have been on a fast-running treadmill most of my adult life and rarely take enough time to reflect on life, family, friendships, and what is important.

This pandemic has been tragic and has caused an even deeper divide in the United States, but there was a silver lining for me. Being naturally extroverted and social I feared that sheltering in place would drive me crazy. In mid-March my wife and I retreated to a small cabin in the North Woods. Apart from a few necessary trips to the big city we are still there. The slow pace, lots of meaningful conversations (some difficult), long walks, and sometimes just sitting silently in front of a burning fire holding hands has brought us so much closer together. We have also become proficient with Zoom and have spent more face time with our kids and grandchildren than when we were living in town.

Old friendships have been rekindled through long phone calls, letters, and Zoom happy hours. I sincerely hope the pandemic wanes in 2021 but will strive to retain my slower pace, and more intimate relationships.

-Bob H. 1954

History will eventually weigh in on the good, the bad, and the ugly of 2020!

The year started with hope and anticipation but soon went in the ditch as 3 major storms converged around us: COVID-19, social justice, and a presidential election, each with a distinctive life, and yet powerful overlapping turbulence.

Today we are still in the storm, so it is difficult to rationally access the full impact. The storms have ripped apart the very fabric of personal, family, business, and societal norms. We are left grieving what we have lost with only hope and uncertainty as to the future.

Flexibility, agility, creativity, innovation, and a sense of humor have been and will continue to be critical to holding our own and redefining the future. Many are experiencing stress in all aspects of our lives. Personal situations (health, financial, etc.) impact how we cope. Weaknesses are exaggerated while strengths afford cushion to the stress. It feels as though we are grieving what has been lost without clarity as to the future.

I am fortunate to have a solid foundation that has provided strength throughout the year. We live in a remote area where social distancing has been easy and safe. I am blessed that my family is in good health and in some ways closer than before.

I have heard it said that you learn the true nature of people (individuals and societies) in adverse times. I am confident we will rally and be stronger for coming through the storms.

-Bob K. 1954

My dad was born in 1912. He was in first grade in 1918 when the flu epidemic came. In his class of 12, 4 died from the flu. His mother died in her 40's, leaving her sons 12 and 17 with a widowed father. They had no antibiotics to cure infection, no vaccines to prevent disease, no respirators. Appendicitis was a common and fatal infection.

My childhood was a time of relative peace. We got the polio vaccine in the early 1950's which was felt to be a miracle. Today's scientists have computers, electron microscopes, and scientific tools that Jonas Salk could never have even dreamed of. Today the coronavirus will be conquered soon, thanks to our brilliant scientists.

My profession gave me many gifts—mainly the gift of trust. I have had the privilege of helping people through times of overwhelming grief, and times of overwhelming joy. That trust is priceless, and I will forever cherish it. Every day I thank my Creator for the life given me. Nothing can take me down as long as I focus on my gifts, and my joy.

A quote from my daily reader:

"I am a spiritual creature, capable of faith, hope, and an appreciation of beauty. I have an unlimited source of strength and comfort at my disposal."

I make no room in my heart for fear.

-Bob M. 1947

*I*n this world there are things, events, and/or life itself that I can:

1. Control

2. Influence

3 HAVE NO CONTROL

I choose not to waste any emotion on number 3. I am informed (I seek to understand, but not necessarily agree) and act accordingly. But I leave all my energy for numbers 1 & 2.

In 1 & 2, I focus on gratitude! For with gratitude, any negative attitudes grow weaker and weaker. With gratitude, all my actions are to attract versus repel relationships. With gratitude and a grateful heart, I can be filled with p e a c e and joy.

-Bob W. 1945

There are things I cannot fix, problems I cannot solve. So I am amazed how many of them others can—the scientists, activists, makers, and thinkers among us do amazing things. What humankind can accomplish, takes my breath away. Thank God, treatment and prevention of COVID-19 will be among them soon, I think.

My joy at our progress treating COVID-19 is tempered by the lack of progress I see on other issues. Our capacity for evil seems to me as strong as ever. Really, why is it so much easier to create a vaccine for SARS-CoV-2 than to address racism, hunger, poverty, and corruption? Some say that we could cure these ills too, if we devoted the same money and resources to them. I'm not so sure.

Even at age 73, it is a struggle for me to tell the whole truth sometimes. To love, to forgive, to give and share, to acknowledge my Creator, to do the right thing: these things are hard, often beyond me. I celebrate the accomplishments of women and men and thank God for their capacity to treat COVID-19. And I think we have a responsibility to do good, seek justice and show mercy. My hope to be whole and healthy, and for you to be whole and healthy, rests in the mystery revealed by God, **"Christ in you, the hope of glory."** (Colossians 1:27)

-Bruce D. 1947

My thoughts during the pandemic-induced isolation:

- ☀ I'm so sad for all the furloughed/unemployed people. It will take them forever to rebuild their lives.

- ☀ I feel sad for small business entrepreneurs who have lost everything through no fault of their own.

- ☀ Creamy peanut butter and chunky peanut butter are both great.

- ☀ Zoom is miraculous but thoroughly unsatisfying.

- ☀ In-person visits are precious.

- ☀ Buddy Teitleman has found yet another way to avoid paying back the $12 I foolishly loaned him.

- ☀ The New York Times is amazing.

- ☀ Grocery delivery service is wonderful.

- ☀ I miss wandering the aisles of grocery stores.

- ☀ I'm glad I don't have to make a living selling men's suits.

- ☀ On-demand tv is a gift from the gods.

- ☀ The pandemic's wonderful benefit to me: no longer able to go to the fitness center for exercise.

- ☀ I really miss live theater.

- ☀ When the quarantine ends, how will I remember to pick up my shoes at the shoemaker?

-Burt C. 1930

In reflecting on 2020 and all that is happening around the world, we can think of one word that sums up how we feel:

Grateful

Over the last few years we have gone about our lives in a state of bliss. We have great jobs, we could travel the world, eat out at wonderful restaurants, spend time with family and friends. That all came to a screeching halt in March 2020; and with it, many questions: would our family, friends, and especially our older parents be safe and healthy?

Since the early days of the pandemic, we made a conscious effort to go for daily walks, sometimes twice a day, to help relieve stress. We have reached out to loved ones who live alone to provide comfort, and also participated in daily meditation and prayer. Our faith has remained strong, however, one of the hardest things is not being able to attend mass on Sundays.

What 2020 has shown us is that each day is a gift that can't be taken for granted. And it is the health of family and friends that is truly important. We will remember this time as one that allowed us be closer to the people we love and not take anything for granted, even a hug.

-Carey O. 1976 & Rob M. 1965

Taking this opportunity to reflect on the changes and challenges of 2020 has been an interesting journey.

My thoughts are scattered between heightened awareness of our mortality, frustration and fear about our societal values, and new-found appreciation for family and friends. Change is inevitable but progress, in the current crisis of our national identity and values, is questionable and worrisome.

I worry about the morals, violence, widening differences, and the hatred and isolation that seem to multiply daily. Along with the cure and health of one and all, my hope is that we can find our way to renewing our outlook as a community of individuals and focus on the concepts of country, honor, respect, tolerance and perspective. Perhaps that change starts with each one of us in every personal interaction.

In the technological surge that dominates our society, with all its attendant promises and problems, my wish is that we reclaim simpler lives, a slower pace, decency, tolerance, and respect.

Hopefully all generations, including my grandchildren and beyond, will see the wisdom and rewards of taking time to cherish freedom, to be kind to all, explore nature, and to share their patience, purpose, and passion.

-Carol S. 1951

My life in 2020 was focused on the progress of **Alzheimer's**, a disease I was diagnosed with in June 2019. This transcended my feelings about the COVID-19 pandemic and any concerns that came with it. That does not mean I was careless or did not have empathy for what was happening around the world. It was just that my knowledge of what was real for my future removed the fears I witnessed in others.

I am fortunate to be surrounded and supported by loving friends and family. I describe my husband as my rock and I don't know what I would do without his loving care and attention. It is the journey of Alzheimer's not the pandemic, however, that has created a profound depth of our love and intimacy. A saving grace is also a shared sense of humor, which helps us both every day of our lives.

I accept my disease although I hate my growing inability to do the things that were previously so normal. The frustration often leads to tears and feelings of incompetence. Fortunately, I am able to move through the experience and get to the other side. My natural optimism propels me forward and allows me to make the most of whatever time I have left. I am not afraid of dying, but my heart aches with the thought of leaving those I love.

-Cheryl H. 1946

2020 A year that needs no introduction. It was more than anything a year of reflection. Reflection on what mattered most, what our goals were, who we were and who we wanted to become. Stricken with disagreements on how to handle this time of uncertainty, it was a time that allowed us to learn more about ourselves as individuals and as a newly married couple.

2020 magnified likes and dislikes, and solidified our principles and beliefs. It challenged us to be uncomfortable in our own privilege, and question the privilege of others. It shook us to our core to speak up for ourselves and everyone whose voices were muted or had difficulty expressing the hardships they face from their neighbors, community, and even nation. If our words reached at least one person, that is more than we can ask for.

2020 despite the challenges, also brought a little light into our lives. In an unprecedented time, we were fortunate enough to spend quality time with each other, our first dog (Ragnar), and rescued our new addition (Layla). Besides learning more about ourselves as individuals, we also learned about the give and takes of a relationship. We recognized it takes effort to continue to strengthen the foundation on which our love was built upon.

2020 is a year we will never forget. For through the uncertainty, we've never been more certain of ourselves and our values.

-Christina N-D. 1994 & Viet N-D. 1991

"If we have no peace,
it is because we have
forgotten we belong
to each other."

-Mother Teresa.

Wise words about the abiding value of human connection. During the pandemic this has been a harsh reality, but human connection is what we all must strive for in our lives. Reach out to family and friends, take the time to actually listen, mend fences and lastly, pray.

-Collette C. 1953

Like other people who challenge us to think hard about fundamental matters and even pray about them, St Paul can be irritating. Sometimes we just want to be left **alone**. I've re-inhabited my immediate environment and had more time to process the many struggles of our country and our world. I've read more deeply about American slavery, Reconstruction, and the rise of Jim Crow. But I've also been desperate to go deeper, to get underneath the surface turmoil of the pandemic, natural disasters, elections, and all the fear that these crises generate. I turned to Paul, that maddening genius, who always kept an eye on the cosmic context even as he managed the growing pains of brand-new Christian communities scattered around the Mediterranean.

In his greatest theological and spiritual work, the Letter to the Romans, Paul wrote:

I consider that the sufferings of this present time are not worth comparing with the glory about to be revealed to us…. We know that the whole creation has been groaning in labor pains until now; and not only the creation, but we ourselves, who have the first fruits of the Spirit, groan inwardly while we wait for adoption, the redemption of our bodies. For in hope we were saved. Now hope that is seen is not hope. For who hopes for what is seen? But if we hope for what we do not see, we wait for it with patience. (Rom 8:18, 22-25)

-Columba S. 1957

WHAT TO BELIEVE?

WHO TO BELIEVE?

EVERYONE HAS AN OPINION

FALLING WITH NOTHING TO HOLD ON TO

I FIND MY FEET AGAIN

BY LOOKING AT NATURE

TREES BUDDING

GRASS-GREENING

FLOWERS AWAKENING

BIRDS AND CRITTERS EMERGING

AND GOING ABOUT THEIR DAY

LIFE STILL WENT ON DESPITE
THE HUMAN CRISIS

NATURE KEPT ME FROM MY LOSING MY SANITY

NO MORE NEWS OR NEWSPAPERS

LISTENING POLITELY BUT NOT ENGAGING

IN CONVERSATIONS SURROUNDING THE PANDEMIC OR
POLITICS

FEELING BOTH THE SADNESS AND HAPPINESS AT THE HUMAN
SPIRIT DOING ITS BEST TO SURVIVE

And find its way to being grounded again

-Connie B. 1964

I'm one of the fortunate ones, at least so far.

With the exception that the pandemic has drastically limited the opportunity to visit my dementia-confined wife, my life has not changed that much in these pandemic months. Retired, gratefully in good health, with adequate resources, surrounded and supported by family and friends who seem to worry about my welfare, I consider myself so much more fortunate than many. My loneliness is not necessarily the lack of friends, but by the absence of The Friend.

The isolation has provided opportunity to read more, to reflect more, to make those calls catching up with friends I might not have otherwise. The Love and Friendship of Others has become even more meaningful. And I am thankful for all those who serve during these trying times.

I do grieve and pray for my wife, for all those affected by the pandemic, for the contentious state of our country, for the lack of stewardship of our earth, for the injustice and suffering in the world.

But I also have faith and hope that we will survive the pandemic, that man's better self will emerge, that we and future generations can make the future brighter for all, and that the two Great Commandments of Love will prevail.

-Dale B. 1938

It is the cusp of a new year. Soon we will leave 2020 behind and with it an entirely new opportunity to carry with us the idea of hindsight being 20/20.

One short year ago, I'm fairly confident that I didn't even know what Zoom was. It is now common for me to host three or four Zoom meetings each day and I have an entire project that depended on Zoom to reach hundreds of rural Minnesotans in 2020 with what was designed to be a live theatre experience followed by a community conversation. Successfully reimagining this project for a virtual stage will remain one of the greatest tightropes I walked this year. It appears the virtual version of "The Remember Project" is poised to reach thousands of people in the upper Midwest in 2021. Mind-boggling.

All this time on virtual platforms has raised serious questions for me, at a very deep soul level, yet this time has also helped me see how resilient and creative we humans can be. The most important thing of all is that I've noticed how easy it is to slip away from a fully lived experience—with all our senses—of thinking, feeling, and acting in the real world complete with the sights, smells, and sounds of nature.

-Danette M. 1960

I fear that as I step outside the comfort of my home to go to work, that I may get COVID from my co-workers. I FEAR when I pump gas I may contact the virus on the handle that the person before me left behind. I FEAR that when I go to the grocery store and pick out my fruit I may end up buying the one apple that another has touched who has the virus. I FEAR the person standing in front of me at the check out line. I would have this question in my head "does that person have COVID?" Worse yet, I limit myself from seeing people I care for in FEAR that I may give them the virus since I am still going to work and risk exposing myself to the virus. This virus has brought the FEARS out of me, the FEAR that I never thought I would have to face, since those FEARS really need me to dig deep into my emotion to surface.

On a positive note, COVID-19 has enabled me spend more time with my family. We've had the time to slow way down during this pandemic. No need to rush, everything is moving at a relaxing pace. No need to figure out the weekend plan, where to go for dinner. It is nice to come home after work and just sit around the house and relax because I don't need to do anything. There's nowhere to go!

-Danh T. 1971

The pandemic has given me time to slow down and have better work-life balance. I have cooked more and have cleaned out excess. I have talked with my family. I have taken much better care of myself because I have had more time. I have read many books, relaxed and have had more time to sit and contemplate my life.

There were times of despair at the beginning of the pandemic. A feeling of being alone and not near my family. It was scary, and then it became a way of life that has been nice as far as the time it has allowed me not to spend commuting and working in an office. I can take a walk and be in nature instead of just walking for exercise. Life has slowed down and I have loved it.

I have grieved over losses during this time and am overwhelmed by the number of deaths. I have known people to be sick and die of COVID. To me, it has been incredibly sad. I will honor this time, though, and make the most of it. I think real closeness occurs most reliably, not when pursued or demanded, but when individuals continuously work on themselves. This time has allowed that for me.

-Davia W. 1960

What does this Pandemic mean? I offer this parable:

If life is a meal served in the kitchen of beliefs...

What should be on the table?

Does the range heat with loving hands?

Should the guests be wisely chosen?

Perhaps it is better to set the table for a wayward traveler

With care taken to express tenderness in the preparation

And a smile and toast to the table before you

For the spices chosen are a reflection of the chef

Not for the harmony of the meal, but for the passion in its preparation.

A Toast to MMXX!

-David D. 1967

The year 2020 was a year no one will forget... for countless reasons. One of the TIME Magazine covers in December 2020 portrayed the year 2020 in bold black print, with a large red X across the digits, and below it, the phrase "the worst year ever"

And in many ways, it was.

Yet, in the midst of the brokenness, confusion, chaos, and pain, there were countless stories of courage, of triumph, of blessing, of re-ordering of priorities in life, and genuine joy.

The year 2020 truly brought me both sorrow and great joy: The death of my vibrant 97-year-old mother, and the birth of my first grandchild.

The circle of life. And God is in control of it all.

May we never never give up hope!

-David G. 1955

2020 CAN BEST BE DESCRIBED FOR ME AS BEING IN A TWILIGHT ZONE—A MIXTURE OF THE REAL, SURREAL, AND UNREAL. COVID-19 WAS NOT THE CAUSE, JUST ONE OF THE ELEMENTS.

I ENTERED THE YEAR WITH A PERVASIVE SENSE OF MELANCHOLY. MY WIFE, SIX MONTHS PREVIOUSLY, HAD BEEN DIAGNOSED WITH ALZHEIMER'S AND WE WERE NOW ON A JOURNEY THAT IN SOME WAYS WAS PREDICTABLE, YET HOW QUICKLY THINGS MIGHT PROGRESS WAS COMPLETELY UNCERTAIN.

PRIOR TO THE DIAGNOSIS WE HAD ONLY BEEN MARRIED TWO AND A HALF YEARS. WE WERE BOTH SEVENTY AT THE TIME OF OUR WEDDING AND THE PLAN WAS FOR AN ABUNDANCE OF YEARS AHEAD. MY FIRST WIFE HAD DIED OF OVARIAN CANCER IN 2003 SO IT WAS HARD FOR ME TO GRASP THAT I MIGHT ONCE AGAIN HAVE TO EXPERIENCE THAT LEVEL OF GRIEF.

TWO POSITIVES CAME OUT OF 2020. I WROTE A BOOK AND BECAME AN EXPERT AT LETTING GO. I IMMERSED MYSELF IN LIVING ONE DAY AT A TIME AND SUCCEEDED. I FOCUSED ON MY BLESSINGS AND EXPRESSED GRATITUDE FOR MY GOOD FORTUNE. NEGATIVE PROJECTIONS OF WHAT "MIGHT" HAPPEN WERE DISMISSED WHILE NOT DENYING MY REALITY.

MY PRAYER OR WISH FOR THE FUTURE IS THAT WE WILL KEEP VISIBLE THE MAGNIFICENT EXPRESSIONS OF KINDNESS AND THE BEST OF HUMANITY WE HAVE WITNESSED IN 2020.

-David M. 1946

The year 2020 sounded the call for action for many complacent observers with central focus on personal responsibility. Who could guess that "Mask up, Minnesota!" would mean something so very important?

Although 2020 revealed our Nation as a divided society, a record number of us voted, marched, engaged in public discourse, and listened with an ear for understanding. We paused to empathize with others, and we drew together as family, friends, and neighbors. We sacrificed and donated resources to the greater good. That didn't happen by lucky chance—it was the work of love.

The events of 2020 brought an awakening to us about the fragility of our lives and communities. Neither will stand the test of time without personal engagement in making things better—starting with a focus on the treasures of love, kindness, companionship, and respect for human dignity—even life itself—and the sacrifices that we need to make for the common good.

Change for the social good starts each day we wake up, but we are not alone in this effort. Our first responsibility is to support our family, our community, our nation and, above all, our very humanity. Each day we rededicate ourselves to personal growth and accountability ... and we must act.

So, put on your masks and find a cause that matters ... we have real work to do building a more cohesive community and sharing a fortunate chance to do better.

-Dawn E. 1957 & Chance E. 1956

It all Started with FaceTime...

Beginning in March when we knew we had a serious global pandemic, we all began to explore ways to communicate with other family, friends and business associates. Words like Zoom, Webex, Team, GoTo Meeting, Duo, Gather, to name but a few, pushed their way into our vocabulary!

As we begin 2021, our lives will never be the same because of the pandemic... but hopefully we will use these new technologies to reconnect and stay connected with family and friends now on a more regular basis. I have also used these vehicles to reconnect with people whom I had not talked to or seen in several years! How exciting it has been for me! Sure, we have "bugs" and "lags" with all of these vehicles. We complain... and reconnect... but we continue to use them.

Can you imagine how excited we will all be when we can hug a family member or loved one in person? And never again will we have to say, "virtual hug"— words we will all enjoy saying goodbye to.

-Dean B. 1947

COVID of 2020 has given me a renewed gratefulness, thankfulness and appreciation of God, family, and friends. Life would be empty without them.

A motto I've adopted is:

Do what you can

With what you have

Where you are.

-Delphine D. 1944

The increasing division and lack of compassion among many people this year made me feel very sad and helpless. Now, more than ever, caring for one another is crucial.

Humanity is suffering.

However, if one looks carefully, there are many who continue to care for others quietly, compassionately, respectfully—caring for someone simply because they are a fellow human being. That glimmer of hope, that more kindness and care for one another will return, and sustains me. Join hands and hearts and come together—as humans.

-Diane Ni. 1959

The virus is here to stay. We cannot relax in the face of the pandemic. We must remain vigilant during this unusual time in our lives. We are all in this together, and yes, we all miss our families friends and traditions. I believe the human spirit will reunite us after such divisive times in our world. We must begin to heal our nation. Denial and anger are natural human responses in coping, but we must preach peace, love, and caring for our fellow human beings.

-Diane Nu. 1942

This has been a year of forced transformation. In past times, many of us have survived harships and rebuilt our lives again to what they were. This time so much has changed and or disappeared that my mantra has become:

Build Back Better

It requires more thought and awareness but offers the opportunity to jettison that which was done habitually and often detrimentally or inefficiently.

Time has come to lighten the load, remove the unneeded distractions, and shed contact with negative people and activity that have accumulated like unwelcome clutter.

Now before accepting new tasks or even chores, I ask myself if it is something I desire to do, and will it make me better able to weather the next challenges which seem to be around the next corner.

It seems as if the phrase **"life is constant change"** should be amended to: **"life requires constant reappraisal"**.

-Dick G. 1950

2020, The Pandemic:

✳ We are fine and following the advice of "the experts": Masks, space, washing hands, etc.

✳ Grieving losses: None

✳ Change of Priorities: None

✳ Gifts Received: I can't do anything about what is going on in Washington, but vote and support candidates that I respect.

✳ But I can do things and support others where I live, and that is what I am doing:

    ✳ Jobs and training;

    ✳ Family systems;

    ✳ Education;

    ✳ Affordable housing

✳ My values: Integrity, Respect, Responsibility, Compassion

✳ I am trying to **"Bloom where I was planted."**

-Dick M. 1930

2020 HAS BEEN A VERY DIFFICULT YEAR, A YEAR OF GIVING UP SO MANY ACTIVITIES WITH MY FAMILY AND FRIENDS DUE TO THE CORONAVIRUS PANDEMIC: HAPPY HOURS, LUNCH AND DINNER OUTINGS, BRIDGE CLUB, BUSINESS FUNCTIONS, CHURCH FUNCTIONS, SPORTING EVENTS, FAMILY GATHERINGS, SUMMER VACATION, A NEIGHBOR'S FUNERAL, A FORMER NEIGHBOR'S FUNERAL, A SISTER-IN-LAW'S FUNERAL, A NEPHEW'S FUNERAL, ETC.

BUT ONE THING THAT I HAVEN'T GIVEN UP IS MY FAITH IN GOD. I KNOW THAT SOMETIMES WE DON'T UNDERSTAND WHY GOD DOES WHAT HE DOES. I KNOW THAT GOD DOESN'T SEE THINGS THE WAY WE SEE THEM BUT I HAVE FAITH THAT GOD KNOWS WHY HE DOES WHAT HE DOES— AND THAT HE HAS A GOOD REASON FOR DOING IT.

AS ISIAH 60:22 SAYS, "WHEN THE TIME IS RIGHT, I, THE LORD, WILL MAKE IT HAPPEN."

SO, I AM PUTTING MY TRUST IN GOD.

-Dick P. 1936

I have been finding the current situation here in Wales rather dispiriting, to the point that I find it difficult to generate the right kind of energy for the creativity that I am accustomed to. I am not "doing what I am here to do". Other than general malaise, we are in good shape, with the days flying by with little accountability. I am slowly pulling things together, notwithstanding the low energy levels. "Just put that quill pen in the ink Donald." A lot of support effort for the family has been called upon for almost a year. Closed schools have meant that homeschooling is now the order of the day. If I have been lacking in motivation during lockdowns, the children have been even more challenged. Over time, box-ticking assignments and online assessments leave the kids flagging and without the group momentum of face-to-face communal stimulus — they can feel stranded. Online tuition has been unsatisfactory up until now, with uncertainty between the competing demands of reopening schools with socially distanced, COVID-prepped classrooms and a *Stay home, Save lives*, long-distance learning strategy. So grandfather (me) has been sharing in the task of "pushing rocks up hill" in the education department for some months.

Even so, there has been much valuable learning on offer to all of us in these crises of the pandemic. Frighteningly poor political leadership among Western democracies reveal the fragility of our life on this earth. Time for a reset?

-Donald J. 1938

This current chapter in my life includes the unprecedented experience of the COVID-19 pandemic and the most extraordinary Presidential election. As a "person of a certain age", I could not help but to reflect on how these two important events have affected me. I have had despondent days as a result of the political division in our country, and our democracy being questioned.. We must hope for the best.

I have had several emotional feelings throughout the last eight months, with two that have been most prominent. One is the loss of not seeing the most important people in my life; family and dear friends. Fortunately, the other emotion is one that is positive. I have had some wonderful days of tranquility. I've been blessed financially in retirement; although this blessing does not eradicate one of sorrow for so many that are having a difficult time. Second, and most importantly, I am also blessed with the ability of sharing my life with a wonderful man who brings happiness, shared feelings and peace of mind, especially during isolation.

In the past, I have enjoyed a wonderful life of family, dear friends and travel. That wonderful life, I know, will resume soon, but possibly in a different manner. What the new normal will be, we will all know in time.

-Dorothy N. 1943

2020 It's difficult to describe. A year that feels like a decade. One filled with huge contrasts, complexity and turbulence. A time of 'both and'. As leaders, we are being called on to simultaneously navigate uncertainty and ambiguity in our professional and personal lives in equal measure; slowing down while moving faster, innovating while focusing on the fundamentals, staying in place while transitioning everything, running while standing still.

This time has required an incredible amount of emotional agility and stamina, decision making mettle, courage, adaptation and faith. I've witnessed new depths of all of this in myself, my colleagues, my family and friends and in people across the community. There is an increased sense of altruism, social evolution and shared purpose rising up and uniting us. I'm grateful and inspired by the best in humanity stepping forward and heartbroken and horrified by the worst that has shown up. This duality re-affirms my commitment to the work I do.

-Elizabeth W. 1964

2020 lead me to starting my own business! As a recent college graduate, I had felt pressure to get a full-time job and move to a big city as soon as possible. With COVID limiting my job prospects and cities shutting down, I was able to take a step back and ask myself what really mattered during this down time. Immediately, I gravitated towards my art. I had always enjoyed drawing and painting, but never committed to it, feeling like it wouldn't lead me to a "secure" profession or life.

The silence of the pandemic filled my mind with the noise of new creative visions. A couple months later, I launched my business, where I embroider my art onto a variety of different clothing (an ode to my retail merchandising degree). In total, COVID enabled me to put to rest the unconscious void of societal expectations and awaken the song of my true inner calling. No matter where this business and creative journey may take me, my heart and mind have already thanked me for it.

-Emily E. 1997

I live in New York City. 2020 began with the COVID pandemic soon putting a vibrant city in shutdown and lockdown except for essential workers/caregivers. Three close friends contracted COVID with only "virtual" medical assistance available. Experiencing these changes, I found myself saddened by the suffering and observed expressions of fear and anxiety in voices and actions while we depended more on the internet and email for human contact, humor and creative expression. Concurrently, daily discussions revealed anxiety about our county's political schism. A friend sent me her poem which reflects this:

Brother

He is my brother
He loves this country
He hates politicians
Wheeling and dealing
Waste and corruption.
He loves Trump
And fears for this country
Without him
Because Trump is a businessman
Good for business

He gives his salary to charity
Because he is rich and doesn't need it
No, he has not asked which charities
Nor confirmed the gifts.
It took me a year of explaining
To convince him of global warming.
He is my brother and I need a brother.
I also need honesty, democracy, help
For the needy
transparent governance, dignity,
Set a good example.
We talk carefully.

Yes, I try to remain hopeful for a country experiencing a downsizing, but I struggle to balance pessimism that accompanies this.

-Emily N. 1939

If faith the size of a mustard seed can change the world, can a virus do the same? As a month became months, I was stunned both by the change that came upon me as well as the change that I embraced.

Despite being a monk in a monastery, years of business travel had transformed my life. When all that came to a halt, I wondered if anything could take its place.

My first weeks in isolation were difficult, and I felt as if I were in a minimum security prison. As time went on, however, I realized I had to change my attitude, even if I could not change my physical circumstances. That's when I decided I had been awarded the academic grand prize: a research sabbatical for which I had not applied.

I then set myself to a limited number of tasks. For the first time in years I took part in the full schedule of prayer. I took my turn at serving at table and in cleaning the choir stalls. I began to write all my letters by hand. I tended to my health. Most important of all, I got to know my fellow monks for the first time in years.

Cataract surgery was the capstone, and it opened my eyes both literally and symbolically. With 20/20 vision I realized that life could blossom again. A virus had imprisoned me, but it also caused me to reclaim my life.

-Eric H. 1948

This pandemic has only served to remind me, on a daily basis, of the certainty imparted in an old Irish proverb:

"It is in the shelter of each other that the people live"

-Eric M. 1945

Overall, I'd say my experience with the pandemic has been a unique one. In ways, I feel anger towards it, as I can't see friends and family as much as before the pandemic began, and not being able to go to school in person. But, I think this stretch of what has been the weirdest time of my life has also seen me grow, especially in a mental state.

As a teenager who has been afraid of change his whole life, this change I decided to take on. And I adapted to the change better than I could've ever imagined. I saw myself getting closer with the people I was still allowed to see. I developed routines right when everything started, and I never broke them. I adapted to a new kind of school, and especially, I was able to adapt to a new lifestyle I never thought I could or would live.

Overall, though, I'd say this pandemic was the worst thing that ever happened to me.

But also the best thing that ever happened to me. I wouldn't be half the man I am without the experience I was forced to experience.

-Erik E. 2005

The COVID virus for myself and my family has been an experience like never before. Through these times, we have become closer. Learning about each other and spending even more time together than usual. We've had the great pleasure of trying many new things. I've traveled to new places to experience nature away from the crowds, I've started to read books again, and much, much more. I'm blessed to be able to say that this pandemic has been a great experience for myself and my family when it's been such a burden for others. I'll look back fondly on these memories for the rest of my life.

-Flynn M. 2005

The pandemic has added both positives and negatives to my life. First, the negatives:

- I live in a great community and I used to go to a worship service on Sunday mornings with about 25 other people. Of course, we no longer meet and I miss the connection with the people.
- I spent Thanksgiving by myself—which was a bummer. And will do so at Christmas as well.
- I have found it hard to stay connected to my six kids. If it were not for the pandemic, I would have traveled to each of them for a long weekend or even a couple of weeks.

Now, the positives:

+ I'm a fairly strong introvert, so the pandemic has given me a lot of time to read.
+ While it would be nice to have a deep friendship with a woman—I'm not very hopeful that this will happen. But, one never knows!
+ The pandemic has given me time to ponder my mortality. I find it interesting that I've already outlived the modal expectation for white males. I'm planning on 15 or 20 more! (Optimists do live longer!)
+ I have stayed connected to my six kids with Zoom calls, texts and emails.
+ I have a puppy! She's a small dog (10 lbs)—Shih Tzu and Bichon cross. She's marvelous companion and she takes the edge off loneliness.

I am blessed... I live on 103 pristine acres with abundant fresh air and fascinating wild life.

-Fred K. 1940

Amid tens of millions of COVID-19 cases worldwide and more than a million deaths from the coronavirus pandemic, while self-isolating, quarantining, and sheltering in place, and being unable to hug our parents, children, grandchildren, and friends, I have sustained myself by keeping the center of my attention on hope.

Iris Murdoch, the famous British philosopher and novelist, insisted that "those who hope, by retiring from the world, to earn a holiday from human frailty, in themselves and others, are usually disappointed." Hope arises from a combination of engagement and generosity; in doing "good for nothing."

During the turmoil of the 1960s an editorial in the Christian Century attempted to deal with the grim details of that time with these words:

"We have occasion now to learn something about the context of Christian hope. It is a 'crucified hope,' born in spite of Babel and Golgatha, in the midst of a world sick unto death. It depends not on journalistic optimism or sociological documentation, but on the promise of God. It is a 'resurrected hope,' born in the midst of a world that shows few signs of resurrection, gives no evidence that the new creation has begun, and is always on the verge of happening to us."

Focus on hope.

-Gary R. 1948

God grant us serenity

Doubles, troubles; pollution, revolution; racist, prejudiced; division, despair; delusional, denial; raging, suspecting; demeaning, denying; fear, tear; daring, doubting; collusion, exclusion; scarceness, emptiness; perplexing, obfuscating; Chaotic, despotic; dismissive, defiant; deceit, destruction; oppression, suppression; isolation, desolation; protest, unrest; political, judgemental; fictions, restrictions;

To accept the things we cannot change

Pandemic, pessimistic; cynicism, optimism; challenging, understanding; loneliness, depression; quarantine, byzantine; fraud, contempt; virus, mysterious; darkening, perplexing; painful, shameful; subversion, reversion; egotism, sexism; blind, bizarre;

Courage to change the things we can

Generosity, inclusivity; compassion, conversation; intentional, confidential; remote, smote; viral, tranquil; health, strength; vision, passion; insight, foresight; light, bright; distance, discovery; researching, developing; assurance, compliance; sheltering, Sharing; conscience, science; enlightening, encouraging; bonding, inspiring; friendliness, awareness; fortitude, gratitude; substantive, inventive; positive, peaceful; relationships, friendships; longing, dreaming; non-violence, resistance; profiteers, volunteers;

And wisdom to know the difference

Integration, reconciliation; immigrants, vigilance; medical, practical; humility, tranquility; voicing, rejoicing; brilliance, resilience; integration, restoration; prolific, scientific; quality, equality; heroic, stoic; cooperation, consultation; rebuilding, reordering; respectful, tactful; healing, inspiring; friendliness, awareness; substantive, inventive; wellness, wisdom; positive, peaceful; reassembling, reestablishing; faithful, consequential; responders, wonders; front liners, back liners; family, friends; teachers, parents; doctors, nurses; helpful, hopeful; assertive, Progressive; vetting, voting; reflection, election; trial, vial, serene, vaccine.

-Gene P. 1944

efore the COVID-19 pandemic, I would often look at my overloaded calendar and think, "Stop the world, I want to get off!" But, as they say, "Be careful what you ask for, you just might get it." So here we are. The world is virtually stopped. And we are wondering why so many familiar and well-loved things have been taken away from us.

A sermon I once heard was about "release and receive." The priest told a story about his 2-year-old nephew who had a favorite stuffed animal that he carried around everywhere. Father Sam came for a visit and brought chocolate chip cookies as a treat. He didn't want his nephew to get them all over his beloved toy, so he said to put down the stuffed animal in order to get a cookie. Naturally, the little guy threw a tantrum because he wanted both the toy and the cookie at once.

The priest compared that situation to the experience of loss—loss of control, loss of pleasurable things, or loss of fun experiences with family and friends. Since COVID, we have all had our "toys" taken away, to one degree or another. Perhaps the resulting fear and uncertainty, combined with an over-abundance of idle time, might just be God's invitation to completely change our orientation and make Him the center of our lives rather than a calendar full of activities and a house full of things.

-Gerrie B. 1947

2020 Pandemic thoughts:

* I don't like being locked up or locked down.

* I don't like Government picking winners and losers.

* I miss giving and getting hugs. Human contact is too important.

* Media outlets are a menace to society and sell fear for clicks or ratings.

* Facebook is a virtual sewer with a www address. Best not to swim there.

* White-coat scientists are not deity—they should be questioned.

* Scientific consensus takes many years to achieve.

* This pandemic is creating lifelong hypochondriacs.

* Viruses don't care what political tribe you belong to—they are equal opportunity invaders.

* The economy would be dead without the $4 trillion borrowed from our unborn descendants.

* Stealing from the young and/or future generations to perpetuate the old is wrong. US National debt is at $27+ TRILLION DOLLARS. REMEMBER, the bankers always get paid back in the end.

* The blame game is alive and well. Same as it has always been.

* Government puts the "fun" in the word Dysfunctional.

* Dictatorships handle pandemics better that democracies.

* Mankind's hubris knows no bounds. Everyone has become a virus expert this year.

* There is a God, and I am not him. Everyone gets their ticket punched eventually.

* The virus will win in the end.

-Greg H. 1958

2020 taught me to care and think more about other people. This pandemic forced me to hold my breath to be with the people I love, as gathering could spread the virus. This year has also improved overall communication in many ways, modernizing how we can effectively keep in touch with those who matter most to us.

I'm grateful that Mother Earth was able to take a bit of a break from us this year, as the lockdown meant less pollution from daily commutes.

I'm thankful for all the togetherness and bonding time this year gave me with my growing family.

I'm appreciative the election is now behind us, and pray 2021 and beyond will bring us all hope, healing, and joy.

Thank you 2020 for all your lessons. You are now our history, and a legend for the next generation.

-Hanna S. 1993

The most unusual time of our lives is the COVID-19 epidemic.

At our ages 85 and 84 we have as a team weathered many heartaches and many blessings. So many we cannot remember them all. With 60 years of marriage there have been events and situations that we feel have imparted some degrees of wisdom.

My faith as an ordained Deacon in the Episcopal Church in Minnesota has helped me in almost every aspect of my life to cope and realize that God is always with us. It is this belief, my contact (in person / Zoom) with family, parishioners, and friends that sustains me both mentally and physically. Believing and knowing that life is all circular and not linear and that the native Lakota beliefs are those of the ages which overshadows all of humanity is a true blessing.

I am not able to pinpoint one or even two particular events that stand out as life changing. However, the elections, the polarization of our lives and threats to our democratic way of life affect all of us, regardless of our individual political beliefs, family beliefs, faith beliefs, or actions.

W'oniyaken Toksa

-Harlan S. 1935 & Beth S. 1936

In our 45 years of marriage, we have learned a happy life is dependent on:

#1. Unconditional Love
#2. Good Health
#3. Time Together

The virus has regrettably compromised #2, the Health of many people. And, unfortunately, the virus has greatly reduced #3, Time Together. But, in spite of its best efforts, the virus is incapable of harming the Unconditional Love we feel for family and friends. That will be eternal.

Both of us have a positive view of the future. Even though the virus is reducing the Time Together we have remaining, it is not capable of eliminating our wonderful memories.

We know there are better days ahead.

-Harvey B. 1944 & Bev B. 1943

In spite of high levels of power, wealth, progress in physical sciences, and technology attained by the U.S. and other countries, we still experience extraordinary failures and suffering. The pandemic and other international and national crises have increased division, violence, racism, sickness and death. This decade is considered lost for the global economy by the World Bank, and, according to Sir David Attenborough is our last opportunity to prevent irreversible damage to the natural world and collapsing societies.

Einstein and other physicists warned about the pitfall of technological communication outpacing human communication. A key to reestablish balance is education. In the context of our crisis over democracy and freedom, Jefferson wrote that educating the whole of the people is essential since "We the People" are the only sure reliance for the preservation of liberty. A fundamental vehicle of education is communication. Benjamin Franklin believed schools, along with parents and community, are responsible for building character and wisdom, but schools have recently focused mainly on knowledge. British philosopher Nicholas Maxwell has proposed over three decades that education must refocus toward wisdom inquiry.

-Hector G. 1943

We re-learned the importance of:

1. Purpose, meaningful work

2. Health

3. Hope

4. Patience

5. Gratitude

6. An afternoon nap

7. A walk with no place to go

8. And most importantly, our faith, family and friends.

-Helen R. 1949 & Jim R. 1949

The most disappointing thing this year has been the lack of U.S. concern regarding the transmission of the virus and potential results. We have closely followed CDC recommendations due to age, Jack's diabetes, and our strong desire to not unintentionally pass the virus to others.

Greatest personal losses have been the inability to have face-to-face meetings with others for birthdays, anniversaries, graduations, church, funerals, sports events, cocktails/dinner, and sitting around the "liar's fire" after fishing with friends. We have also grieved the death of many friends and acquaintances during this time (not from the virus) and funerals have been put on hold.

Priorities have not been re-aligned, simply strengthened. We are more aware of the needs of others—fellowship, food, education, jobs, etc. Our family relationships have been strengthened as we have worked together to protect each other from this pandemic. We have spent more time sanitizing things and cooking meals at home.

Most significant blessing is that we and our friends have been free of COVID hospitalization. Those who have tested positive did appropriate quarantines and re-tests. Our faith strengthened, knowing God is in control of everything.

-Jack C. 1943 & Sheila C. 1942

From the moment I first learned of its impact on people's behavior, I realized it would be at least as significant as the stock market crash of 1929 and the great depression. It's a reminder of how rapidly and unexpectedly the world can change and the need for us to play the hand we've been dealt.

Now some 10 months later, as vaccines are being developed and administered, there is hope for recovery. I have personal health challenges that add to questions about the near term future.

Through it all I've tried to "let go and let God". I've been blessed in so many ways.

-Jack S. 1936

As I reflect on 2020, I am reminded of something the character Emily said in the play, Our Town.

> *"It goes so fast. We don't have time to look at one another. I didn't realize. So all that was going on and we never noticed... Wait! One more look. Good-bye world. Good-bye, Grover's Corners...* Mama and Papa. Good-bye to clocks ticking... and Mama's sunflowers. And food and coffee. And new ironed dresses and hot baths... and sleeping and waking up. Oh, earth, you are too wonderful for anybody to realize you. Do any human beings ever realize life while they live it—every, every minute?"

There were so many good-byes in 2020 and so many things I took for granted. So many celebrations cancelled. So many gatherings evaporated. Good-bye to my mom's beef stroganoff at Christmas dinner. Good-bye dancing with my crazy Irish cousins in the St. Patty's Day Parade in downtown St Paul. Good-bye weekly hugs at mass at St. Joan of Arc. Good-bye watching a Twins Game at Target stadium. Good-bye baby showers and weddings and Happy Hours with friends. I didn't realize how many things I loved until they were gone...

-Jane C. 1962

"It's a God Thing"

Emotions and feelings in 2020 were extreme for me.

The peaks and valleys were at their highest and lowest.

The rivers and streams ran deeper with a lot more rocks in the way to challenge the journey.

<u>Daily Affirmations I tell myself to be my best self:</u>

• Be open to those experiences which can only be explained as, "It's a God thing."

• Always listen from the inside to your "God voice."

• Count your blessings when you wake up, AND when you go to sleep.

• Stay connected with those you love and who love you.

• Be thankful for your wonderful life with your loving soulmate.

• Be grateful for your musical talents in bringing people together to share the joy and transformative power of music. It's a rare gift.

When I was about eight years old, I asked my beloved Mama a question. "Mama, so many people love you. How can you have so much love to give back?" She replied with a smile, "Honey, you never run out of love. God gives you an endless supply."

-Jeanie B. 1951

On March 17, 2020—the news came to all of us in Minnesota that we were to vacate our work space and shelter in our homes. Within a few days, 300 people in my office began working remotely. Fear gripped everyone as the thought of a shutdown would clearly effect our clients and our business. My firm took a wise and very conservative path to reduce cash outflow significantly, as a means to weather the potential storm.

As I moved from St. Paul to northern Wisconsin to be with my wife, we were concerned, scared and searched for answers that were hard to come by.

What clearly changed my perspective was a call from a Deacon friend during the earliest weeks of the pandemic. He stated candidly that he was praying for me—but the prayers were to turn my worries to God—which he said would be hard for me to do. In the end he said God would be in charge. Over the weeks and months, it was clear to me that others needed to rely on me, as I needed to rely on God that we would get through this together. My faith increased, and my understanding of the trials to strengthen my faith came hard but were the best lessons I could learn. Psalm 56:3—

When I am afraid, I put my trust in You.

-Jeff D. 1963

COVID opened our eyes to much.

We learned it really is necessary to prepare for a national emergency. We now have food supplies and life basics stowed for the next rainy day.

We moved fast to answer a short notice calling to remove a parent (with a hearing impairment and memory loss) from independent living into our small home over the course of a year. We learned much about memory loss and the hardships one encounters caring for an elderly parent at home.

We needed exercise and fresh air to maintain our mental health so we started a large DIY landscaping project in our yard. This provided purpose and a break from the sadness COVID was inflicting on people in our country and in the world.

We experienced friends who got the virus and quickly got well. We lost an older loved one who caught it and their already deficient immune system succumbed to the COVID virus. We count our blessings every day we personally have stayed safe from COVID and we pray for those who have lost so much life and livelihood from this pandemic.

2020 showed us that things we used to take for granted in Seattle, we no longer can count on. For us, 2021 promises to be a year of reflection and change.

-Jeff N. 1958 & Alicia N. 1960

Over the course of this pandemic, I learned the true value of human touch. Working as a RN through this pandemic, in a senior living community, I saw first hand the significance of caring touch, whether that be an arm rub, hug, or hand hold. Human contact is vital to emotional, social, and physical support.

With the pandemic, however, I found myself questioning something I used to give so freely. I can see the look of confusion, disappointment, and longing when I pass my residents and cannot give them that same personal involvement they were accustomed to. So if I had one thing to take away from this pandemic, it would be to never underestimate the significance and importance of caring touch.

-Jennifer D. 1995

ノスタルジック

Natsukashii

To keep fond memories close to my heart.

A feeling of nostalgia embraced in all five senses.

Reliving happy memories of the past.

Warm feelings of appreciation for people and events.

Connections with people and loving memories.

-Jennifer M. 1972

2020 has been amazing. Formerly, I traveled 350-400 thousand miles per year, forever. I have not been on an airplane since February 29th, 2020. I have now learned that I can lead a great company from my home and do it very effectively and efficiently. I communicate with our 8500 colleagues daily. We have had a record year with all working from home. Every colleague has a better work-life balance and in my case I'm in the best physical shape I have been in for years. It is a joy to be with Mary Joy every night and have MJ-and-Jerre-Time every day

-Jerre S. 1943

God's challenge to humanity: The 2020 Pandemic.

It's fair to say that challenges are a part of life so we've tried to stay grounded. It helps us ride the emotional rollercoaster. During a seemingly insurmountable crisis like COVID-19 that threatens our lives and those of others we know and love, our individual actions, we believe, need to inspire others, not frighten them. But give hope. Tomorrow isn't promised to anyone—it may be helpful to lead one's life with this in mind because adversity doesn't build character—**it just reveals it.**

The manner in which we, as individuals and society, respond to COVID says much about our social intelligence. Throughout our lives we're faced with losing friends and loved ones, an outcome comparable to that which COVID can deliver. Nonetheless, the existential nature of this disease with its uncertainty and the unsatisfying answers surrounding it, seems to disproportionately set us off. For us, we turn to a higher being for support and satisfaction.

-Jerry H. 1941

N o one knows what the future will be, especially during these trying times. We as a people hope and pray that we will be healthy, successful, and remain positive in our attitudes toward our future. This requires staying informed and updated on changes in the culture of our country.

We are a capitalist country and that is what made us great! Those individuals who implement Socialism as the theory, and when enacted, becomes Communism! You cannot name a country where Socialism has been successful, not one! Those individuals who espouse this are supposed to be knowledgeable. Confucius also once said, "Real knowledge is knowing the extent of one's ignorance."

-Jerry J. 1936

What strikes us the most during this dreadful pandemic is the lack of touch. No hugs, kisses, hand shakes, or pats on the back. And what is scary: they may never come back.

We are social animals and this lack of human touch is, besides the deaths and illnesses, probably the most lasting and distressing outcome.

Pray the gift of touch returns to our lives.

-Jerry N. 1935 & JoAnn N. 1935

People seem to be at their best during crisis. It is no exaggeration to describe our present as a pandemic-crisis. In so many ways people have been surprisingly caring, giving, helpful. We see this among children as well as strangers.

Ironically, the practice of keeping six feet apart has brought us closer together. We've come to realize how dependent we are on people with more menial jobs. How we need them and miss them.

When I was drafted and dressed in Army uniform, there was an immediate camaraderie. Life-long friendships developed. "All for one and one for all." We were not strangers for very long. "He ain't heavy, Father, He's my brother." Wearing masks is our present uniform, and yes, we're all in this together.

Although church attendance has waned, we look more to the heavens. Sweatshirts read "FAITH OVER FEAR," "PRAY AND LET GOD WORRY." And Peter Marshall wrote: "God will not permit any troubles to come upon us unless He has a specific plan by which great blessings can come out of the difficulty."

We all know that "virtue is made strong in adversity." And over the door of a weight room we read "no pain, no gain." We are inspired by heroic medical people, the quick discovery of vaccine to fight this killer. And compassion pours out at every funeral. People grieve together; people are good at heart. Again, crises brings out the best in people.

As our currency reads: IN GOD WE TRUST.

-Jim Be. 1924

Nancy has been dealing with a treatment regimen of chemo infusions and pills, surgeries, and radiation since 2018. Her medical appointments, and hospital and rehab stays have been too numerous to count. These challenges have given us emotional callouses that have made 2020 easier to tolerate.

Fairly early in the treatment process, we adopted a one-day-at-a-time philosophy. We decided not to waste our energy on what could lie ahead. Instead, we embrace today! We have enjoyed sunrises and sunsets, the springtime explosion of color in crabapple blossoms, the young stag eating the crabapples in the fall, the softly falling flakes of the first snowfall, and the other seasonal wonders that are part of living in Minnesota.

We also celebrate the routine events of each day—morning coffee, tea, and paper, lunch together, computer searches, books, naps, quiet time, tasty dinners and more. Just being together is special.

We have experienced a wonderful role reversal with our three girls and their families. They more and more are directing and helping us deal with the difficult situations that are part of our lives. Love flows freely throughout our family.

Frank Capra said it best, "It's A Wonderful Life".

-Jim Br. 1937 & Nancy B. 1938

*W*ith the winter's darkness I decided that having my furniture arranged around the coffee table and the TV set looking into a dark room was depressing, so I rearranged my furniture so they faced looking outside through the bay window. I grew up with front porches and miss the view they have of the neighborhood and the interactions that took place with the neighbors.

Now a days it seems like porches are in the back of the house with yards surrounded by six-foot fences. I hadn't realized all I was missing. I now know who belongs in my neighborhood, not necessarily their names but certainly who belongs to what breed of dog and what groupings of children. I may be imagining it, but it seems since the COVID lockdown I see more families out walking together. As I sit in my window I get the occasional wave from passersby, especially, the kids; they see everything. Adults see uniforms, but kids see people.

I'm looking into having a front porch built onto my house. During the Trump presidency and the COVID crisis I have become addicted to 24 hour news.They call it doom scrolling. I pay almost $250 a month to be stressed out and depressed watching news. It costs almost nothing to look out my window and be happy. We do make strange choices.

This is my two-cents.

-Jim D. 1949

Somewhere toward the middle of that covid-marked year, I began to hear the insistent whisper of a single word: balance. It came to mind at odd times of the day, and crept into my dreams at night. Eventually, I got the message.

I saw that I had allowed parts of my life to get out of whack—too many Zoom meetings, not enough walks in the woods with a dog. Too much of just money-earning work, not enough of the spirit-lifting kind. Too many rolls of toilet paper stored in my art studio, not enough painting going on.

The pandemic underscored just how fragile this life is, and I am paying attention. For 2021, I've set in motion some much-needed changes. Serenity hangs in the balance.

-Jim M. 1944

I t is an unusual time, to be sure. What we are experiencing is one of those transition periods in history. NPR's Krista Tippit has written, "We are in a communal collective, global transition... moving from one reality to another that we can't see. Part of the work, the calling now is to stand really respectfully before how very unsettling and stress-filled this is."

A major part of the "unsettling" is spiritual. How do we cope spiritually during this time?

First, we cope by processing our corporate hurt and suffering, and we do this by seeking a more intense connection with God, our families and with our faith communities. When we are experiencing grief we need the assurance of the familiar institutions in our lives.

Second, we cope via a renewed quest for meaning in life. What is important in life? Tragedy and suffering always takes us back to the basics. In the words of the Greatest Commandment, the basics are to love God and to love one another.

Third, we cope by expressing our righteous indignation over what has befallen us. Anger is an appropriate response to what we are going through. Like many of you, we have wondered how the wealthiest nation on earth could be so unprepared for a virus pandemic.

More than these, however, we cope because we have hope. Our faith is centered in hope. "Who shall separate us from the love of Christ?" asks the Apostle Paul. In brief, nothing.

-Jim N. 1949 & Elizabeth N. 1947

"Don't it always seem to go
That you don't know what you've got till it's gone?"

This famous Joni Mitchell stanza captures the real wisdom of a pandemic. So, what was my "got" that was gone in 2020?

Naked Faces
My daily walk of shame throughout the pandemic was (and is) arriving at the door of a store and walking back to the car for my forgotten mask. Homer Simpson's "Doh!" comes to mind.

Last Minute Get Togethers
COVID turned a simple, "Hey, you want to come over?" into "We'd like to see you but understand that you plan to see your grandkids in 5.8 days so perhaps the timing is not good—but if it is OK—we can meet on our patio spaced 10.5 feet apart and yes it will be 5 below zero but we have blankets, a fire, and Maker's Mark. Of course, if you don't feel comfortable ..."

Crowded Bars
As I got older, I began avoiding those bars that Yogi Berra described as, "Nobody goes there anymore. It's too crowded." What I wouldn't give for a jam-packed bar with a good band.

But these were worthwhile sacrifices. My childhood friend from New Jersey—a picture of health throughout his life—has been in the hospital with COVID for almost two months. He is starting to turn the corner but there were days when Joni's words were all too real. Lesson learned.

-Jim T. 1958

We've just spent the most bizarre, unsettling year of our lifetimes and I don't believe we've emerged on the other side. I'm pretty sure we've got more crap ahead of us. That being said, in retrospect, 2020 was a year in which I learned to alter expectations, do everyday things in a completely different way, and marvel at how some people can be really stupid, and others truly heroic. I cannot say the pandemic strengthened family relationships... they were already strong.

However, we did make sure to reach out more regularly. Conversations were longer and deeper. My wonderful husband stayed wonderful and we just adjusted to staying home 24/7. If you can max out Netflix and Amazon Prime, then I think we came close.

I never felt isolated or in despair. I never participated in the screaming hysteria about masks and social distancing that I saw others doing. We wear our masks and stay socially distant when appropriate, but never understood the self-righteous indignation others felt obliged to inflict on their fellow citizens.

Although the virus always loomed, we were extremely blessed that it hasn't directly touched us or our families. People we knew got it and suffered greatly, but except for one instance, nobody we know died from it. Like everyone else, I want this to be over. But whenever that happens, I do know that I will never feel entirely safe again. That's perhaps the most lasting damage the virus has done to me.

-Jo-Ann Z. 1952

"We plan, God laughs."

Perhaps that is the bumper sticker wisdom of 2020. I have found that so much of what I had decided, desired, and dreamed became like autumn leaves on a windy day. Everything was in proper place and moving down the path as planned. And then, God laughed. Or perhaps more theologically sound, life happened and life laughed.

For me, this past year was a sacred lesson in adaptability, in trust and in letting go of my many expectations and important plans. At times, this past year, life brought sorrow and suffering to me and to many, and at times, it brought joy and awe. God didn't laugh perhaps but maybe smiled — as an unplanned life began anew.

-Joe C. 1958

The past year, 2020, in China has been an extremely uncommon year. The COVID-19 pandemic dramatically affected our lives. I had to work at home for a month and even after resumption, business travel was limited. Thus, I was thrown back home, facing my 12-year-old son and wife who often complains about my absence in parenting. By sharing more housework and giving more tutoring to my son, I am delighted to find that the quality time with my family has greatly increased and the relationship between my wife and I has amazingly improved.

Another big change is in my job as I start to report to a manager who is new to the company and does things in a very different way. It is very challenging and I had a hard time adjusting to his style of working. "Embrace the change", is what I have been telling myself. Seeing from another perspective, this change is actually a good opportunity for me to learn something new. Meanwhile, I insist on doing what I believe is right, among which, practicing "Servant Leadership"—offering others adequate support—is still my work ethic.

Positive attitude is powerful. We cannot take control of everything. For those out of our control, we should have an easy mind and let it go. Focus on what we can make a change. Positive attitude will help us go through the hardest time and lead toward an enlightened life. And I believe eventually there will be good outcomes.

-Joe H. 1978

When I took food to the homeless encampment across the street at Thanksgiving, I got the opportunity to testify. My testimony was about walking into a pastor's office of a church six years ago and asking her for food. She offered me a seat, gave me a $20 gift card, a cab voucher, and an invitation to visit the church that Sunday. I later joined her congregation. That changed my life!

I cannot give everyone who needs it a gift card (I wish I could), but I did give a $20 Safeway card to a women across the street, with gratitude and in honor of the pastor, whom I consider a true woman of God.

In this pandemic, I've been able to connect over and over with the teachings of that pastor who lives in Minnesota (I'm now in California). For I overcame the challenge of that once in a lifetime event by the greatest app in my life: **Love.**

-Joe W. 1949

Hope rather than fear!

It is so easy to let one's day be controlled by the news media. This reinforces the fear aspect of today's life. But then there is hope—and how that encourages me to be proactive. We have tried to take more of the initiative in communicating with weekly family zoom calls to catch up. Zoom calls have also included reading books with our younger grandchildren, baking Christmas cookies, celebrating birthdays, and special holidays. In some ways we are communicating better and more often than before the pandemic. Personally this change of lifestyle forced by COVID-19 has reinforced in me the importance of family, friends and faith. Watching mass online is quite different, but also provides a time for purpose and reflection—maybe even more than actually being in church. We have found meaningful ways to connect with friends—calling and texting more often, or meeting outside for a glass of wine while social distancing.

I will be forever grateful to the real heroes: the health care workers, the police, fire crews, and first responders. I am concerned, though, how the gap between the wealthy and the less fortunate has widened. I am concerned about the impact distance learning has had on my grandchildren—and all children. As we move forward we will be better or worse—not the same—from our experiences. I pray we will be better.

-John B. 1945

THE PANDEMIC HAS NOT BEEN MY FRIEND.

Having moved into a new community the day the restrictions started has severely limited renewing old friendships and developing new ones. Apart from an occasional visit with a few relatives, my usual family connections have been severely curtailed. The postponement of family gatherings leaves me with lingering doubts about future family unity.

I miss worshipping with my church communities. When we do, the masks manage to dampen emotions and limit the warmth that I treasure. Is it worth going or better to stay safe and try to pray by screen time? Comfort has all but disappeared.

But not all is lost. Zoom has made some relief possible and enjoyable. Face time, which is a new experience for me, has brought delight, seeing up close the smiles and resilience of close friends and nephews and nieces. I am reading more, finding the time and desire to dig deeper into our nation's history. However, the current political drama, if I am wise, will soon require me to "fast' from cable news. Plus, my recent discovery of Netflix is pulling me into its endless orbit. I am considering hiding the remote in my garage until further notice!

I do not know how to grieve the losses I feel. Maybe it's that I am cooking more, sharing the results with some shut-ins and family. And my return to bread-baking gives me a lift. But, another year of pandemic scares the hell out of me. Perhaps that's a good thing! I feel a definite dis-ease with this disease.

-John F.1936

Viewing the Podd Brothers Choral and Orchestral presentation of "How Can I Keep from Singing!", my eyes flood with tears and I am overwhelmed with emotion of the gift of human community, the beauty and diversity of human faces, the sound of different voices, and the expressiveness of human beings as they bring song to life.

Connection

In normal times, we shake the hands of new acquaintances; we embrace friends and family. Human living is everywhere shaped by our physical connection to each other. Suddenly that is gone—it seems like forever since I have been able to give someone a hug! I know that day will come…

Our Catholic liturgy is sacramental and incarnational. At the abbey, we have long shared the full sign of the Eucharist; consecrated, home-made bread and sacramental wine. As monks, we have treasured this full-bodied expression of the sacrament. The pandemic has reduced us to a simple consecrated host. Surely, this is Eucharist, too, and countless Christians become saints receiving it! Though, we long to receive the full symbol.

Like so many others, as monks we may bemoan not being able to meet in person. At the same time, what would we do without conferencing technologies such as Zoom? My heavens, what a gift these have been during this time of pandemic! New learnings everywhere…

-John K. 1949

For us the most difficult part of these past nine or more months of the 2020 pandemic has been the impact on our family and our gatherings. We are a family of huggers, accustomed to celebrating, sharing, laughing, teasing, and enjoying all 22 of us being together at the same time. When a few of us now do get together in smaller groups, the necessity of social distancing takes away the physical closeness that has been part of our family. Parallel to this is the isolation from our friends and the inability to meet together at restaurants and other such places.

However, we often pause and reflect on how fortunate we really are. God has blessed us with a close and loving family. He has blessed us with many friends. He has blessed us with a beautiful home and lifestyle. Having reached our current age, we know for a fact that God is in charge and all things pass; and this too shall pass.

"To everything there is a season." Ecclesiastes 3:1

-John L. 1941 & Kathryn L. 1942

A full year facing the Coronavirus threat has forced new lifestyles and some new priorities for me and my circle of family and close friends. That the virus just happened to come on top of the fourth year of an era of ultra-Trumpism greatly complicates any response to the question, "How are you feeling today?"

Once the full implications of the Virus were absorbed, like most people, my life turned suddenly more inward as socializing, time formerly devoted to travel, restaurants, movie theaters, and creative events, was replaced by stay-at-home time for gardening, reading, podcast listening, overly-lengthy TV series watching, Zooming, and some individual art projects.

As these everyday life shifts happened, still nagging on my mind is making sense of how a crude-sounding New York City real estate millionaire could strike such a populist chord with 70+ million Americans. Beyond the COVID pandemic, major trends including the internet economy, globalization, climate change, militarized policing, media segmentation, and more are surely causing challenges for many, creating career disruption, economic hardship and definitely public disunity. But this is a moment when smart, well-reasoned, collectively-arrived-at policies (i.e. good governance) should be prevailing over vague calls for unfettered capitalism and "personal freedom." They don't seem to be prevailing!

-John W. 1951

2020 has served as a time for much needed prayer and reflection. While I have not experienced any COVID-related losses on a personal level, the effects of this pandemic from a mental health standpoint should not be diminished or forgotten.

This has been a time of isolation and sadness for many, and I have only recently realized the importance of prioritizing time to focus on my emotional well-being. When at all possible, I try to exercise or take a walk, as I have found nature to be an escape from the harsh reality we find ourselves in, even if it is only a temporary pause. Moments such as watching a group of deer in the woods behind our house or sitting outside as my wife and I enjoy the brisk fall air have taken on greater significance and serve as a blessing for me. These moments are an opportunity to give thanks for our continued health, wellness of our family and time that we get to spend together.

-Justin H. 1979

"With one trifling exception the entire world is made up of Other People"

While the common phrase "what will people think?" was used in hopes of instilling good behavior in children, my Mom was much more concerned about, "how will people feel". Her words of wisdom reminded us that doing nice things for others is the right thing to do and it makes you feel good.

Our society today seems very inwardly focused: it's all about ME! As the coronavirus continues to rage, leaving behind devastating social disruption in job loss, homelessness, changes to teaching and learning, affecting future skills that are needed for global health and welfare.

Sheltering-in-place gave many people the opportunity to spend more time with their own family unit. Yes, we miss eating out, professional sports, and youth sports—not just for entertainment but for life lessons learned about sharing and supporting one another as team players.

As we do things for others in our neighborhood, our community, our country and our world, may we be mindful of the difference that will make in the recipient and in the giver. We will get through this and we will do it better if we are willing to rely on each other. For many, what we are experiencing now is an inconvenience, For others who have lost loved-ones or who have been forced into poverty, it is life-changing with an uncertain future. What will we learn from this? Will we begin to look outward?

-Karel W. 1942

We, our children and grandchildren, and our friends and families are well, which is remarkable in this time of COVID-19. We are so grateful. We may not know how to cope with 2020, but we do know that we must look for bright glimmers of hope in the people and events around us. Our thoughts:

Courage. We find ourselves in awe of the courageous people who have become the helpers: doctors, nurses, first responders, grocery worker. How fortunate we are for their courage.

Opportunity. We see great examples of people who have found opportunities to be kind, gentle and giving to us and others. It helps us to know that there is more kindness in the world than selfishness.

Valiant. We know so many people are trying hard to weather these unsettling and difficult times. We pray all will find comfort, shelter, food, patience, peace, and calm. Help us to be valiant in these uncertain times.

Inventive. We marvel at how inventive people have become, finding new ways to learn, create, find laughter, spread joy, and be up-beat. Thank goodness God gave us such inventive brains!

Determination. We are determined to be positive in a time when it is so easy to become discouraged; to be hopeful in a time that seems so hopeless, and to know, finally, that God is watching over us. Isn't that what faith is all about?

-Karmen G. 1950 & Steve G. 1949

*R*etiring from work in November was one of the easiest big-decisions I can remember making. And I can thank the pandemic for that. It has reminded me how much I cherish my loved ones and how truly precious the little time we have together is—to live in the moment with them; to listen, really listen to their words, thoughts and feelings; to not waste precious time thinking about a trip or adventure, but to do it; to not talk about meeting for coffee but actually do it; to make that call, do that thing...

I will not put off the extraordianry adventures, or the ordinary coffees. I will live my life like I am running out of time, because I am. We all are. And I thank the pandemic for reminding me of that!

-Kent L. 1955

Lessons from 2020

The impact of a virus on our wellbeing extends way beyond the disease impacting the vulnerable. It is devastating to witness the results of scientific misinformation and a political spin of COVID reports. The resultant fears of most will extend to many unintended consequences yet to come. But with this, thriving and surviving depend on two simple actions:

Turn off the news,

and

The best healing and nurturing balm for our person and soul comes from exploring and just spending quiet time in the outdoors. There is nothing better for our health than to move and nothing better for our soul than to experience the wonders of the natural world. Beauty, simplicity, intricacy, and the permanence of change are all around us. Discovery of these special moments always leaves one with a profound sense of gratefulness, thanksgiving, and much needed peace.

-Kerry O. 1950 & Carole O. 1950

Early in the pandemic, April 17, 2020 to be exact, was a long day. I was alone in our too-big-for-me home on Cedar Lake in Minneapolis. My spouse and son were COVID-stranded in Bogota, Colombia. A quiet, dark house with a solitary, sleepy and a bit empty occupant. I climbed upstairs to take a moment to relax. I fell asleep... deeper than deep sleep.

Unknown to me, I got up and stumbled towards the intended sleeping room, tumbling head-first over a railing 15 feet high. A direct hit to the head opening a "Y" shaped wound 15-18 inches long. The hardwood floors were not so kind, shattering 22 bones in my neck, back and nearly all ribs on the right side.

Somehow, I do not know how, I re-climbed the stairs and collapsed into a cozy bedroom. While I was unconscious, I was likely fading away... loss of blood alone was life threatening and heart attack inducing. So, what happened? In my slipping-away state, a feeling (not a thought or a voice), revealed itself through the darkness and woke me up. The feeling had an unspoken and undebatable message: LIVE!

This inspired impulse—call it what you want—saved my life. Seven months later I am grateful for this "whack on the head." Sometimes it takes a lot to appreciate the preciousness of life. And, I'm especially grateful to intimately know an essence of life that knows no fear, knows no pain, only knows LIVE!

-Kevin K. 1951

Yes, it's been quite a year. At this writing, thankfully, and amazingly, I've lost no close friends or family to the coronavirus; a blessing I don't take for granted as we head into a new surge upon a surge.

I live alone, work from home, and heretofore, treasured my solitude. When the whole thing began last spring, I thought a few weeks of social distancing might be a bit of an introvert's holiday. I'm long over that. I miss the buzz of a coffee shop, the warmth of human touch, and the bottom two-thirds of human faces.

Three things strike me at this time:

1. How my immense privilege as a straight, white, educated, suburban, currently-healthy, currently-able, cisgendered, well-fed male has allowed me to ride this out with a degree of security and safety that so many—and especially those who are taking care of the privileged classes—can only wish for.
2. How grateful I am that kind, intelligent, honest help is on the way on January 20, 2021!!
3. How I must make the most of every interaction. My human contact has been cut by nearly 90%. The only way I can possibly make sense of it is to be ten times more kind, positive and generous with every human person I run across.

I pray these lessons remain long after the virus has subsided. May we never find a vaccine against our need to love and be loved by each other.

-Kevin L. 1956

During this year, I was both gifted with an extraordinary opportunity to further my career, as well as obstacles that challenged my relationships. My family bond has strengthened because of the pandemic as we have chosen to live a life of solitude and not put any risk on our household. We have grown closer and learned to enjoy our time together. This was also a double-edged sword as it had strained relationships that were hard to maintain outside the household. It has taught me that relationship with another person is fragile and can be put to the test if not fostered correctly.

-Kyle T. 1996

Part 1: As it relates to what the pandemic did *to me:*

The pandemic seemed like the catalyst that set off the perfect storm of life altering events: like the killing of George Floyd. Racism, political divisiveness, and poor national leadership were all brought into our lives by a "Breaking News!" media to grab our attention. Unfortunately, with time on my hands, I drank the "Kool aid" and got hooked on news that seemed more like entertainment. So, to answer what the pandemic did to me? Sad to say, it made me a bit angry and cynical. Usually, I'm a positive, glass half full person but I must admit that I've been negatively impacted by what I've seen. It made me confront a truth I learned many years ago in the Bible in Jeremiah 2:5 *"They followed worthless idols and became worthless themselves"*. Bottom-line, I'm concerned that this time period has lowered the standard of character-based leadership in our country.

Part 2: As it relates to what it has done *for me:*

I have an overwhelming sense of gratitude that our family has been spared the challenges that so many face. While all our family has faced change and inconvenience, we are blessed to be together, healthy, and relatively unscathed. On a personal note, I feel confident that God is in charge and pray positive things will come from this unique time in history.

-Larry J. 1953

DURING THIS PANDEMIC, I GOT INTO HEALING CRYSTALS AND I WISH I WOULD HAVE DONE THIS SOONER. I WAS REALLY ABLE TO REALIGN MY ENERGY TO THE RIGHT THINGS/PEOPLE AND HEAL FROM PAST TRAUMA. IF THERE IS ONE THING I WANT OTHERS TO REMEMBER IT IS THAT "EVERY JOURNEY HAS ITS OWN BEAUTY," AND "EVERYTHING HAPPENS FOR A REASON." ALTHOUGH CERTAIN TIMES MAY FEEL HARDER THAN OTHERS, WE ALL HAVE OUR UNIQUE PATH AND PURPOSE.

-Lauren P. 2000

$\mathcal{A}$t the start, I found myself seesawing between a state of denial and one of fascination—that our global community could be so perilously close to extinction not caused by the usual suspects: nuclear annihilation, military warfare, etc.

That was followed by an over-abundance of optimism that the pandemic would be scientifically resolved by summer. In July, I made peace with restrictions, travel bans, social inconveniences, and began to appreciate free time gained by (1) not working, (2) not having excuses to procrastinate, (3) not having to rush. So, I began to:

✳ Walk, garden, plant, notice my environment more.
✳ Appreciate our home as a true sanctuary.
✳ Feed and study birds that visit our 9 feeders.
✳ Pay more attention to the unmet needs in our Twin Cities community and realize how my own zip code comfort contributes to the inequities of education, economy and social injustice and unrest that was magnified by the George Floyd murder.
✳ Read about racism, antiracism.
✳ Reach out to long lost friends.
✳ Read obituaries ...and appreciate how fleeting and precious life is.
✳ Re-contemplate the difference between NEED and WANT.
✳ Understand that we are all human and we all need to be loved, understood, appreciated and heard.
✳ Be grateful for good health, for my husband/companion, Mike, our family, for a functioning (mostly) democracy.

-Linda M. 1952

How do I live with COVID-19?

A Time will come... our time has come. How do we receive this COVID-19 time as an invitation to go into the inner room of our hearts and love the Stranger?

F or me this Stranger is my Divine Self, my True Self, My True Essence. This time continues to be a peeling away of the old false images of the self or ego. There is an invitation to release my identity found in my busyness, my accomplishments, successes, projects, etc. It is a contemplative time of greeting the True Self that beckons me to "Sit Here...Eat...Feast on my life."

Love After Love by Dale Wolcott

The time will come. The day will come.
The day will come when with elation
   You will greet yourself arriving at your own door,
   And each will smile at the other's welcome saying-
   Sit here, eat.
You will love again the stranger who was yourself.
Give wine. Give bread.
Give back your heart to itself to the stranger who has
   Loved you all your life,
   Whom you ignored for another,
   Who knows you by heart.
Take down the love letters from the book shelf,
   The photographs, the desperate notes.
Peel your own image from the mirror.
Sit. Feast on your life!

-Linda W. 1947

The gifts no one wants

That's how I've come to think of the immense blessings my last few years of losses and struggles have brought—pre-pandemic—and a phrase that's been running through my head a lot in these days of quarantine. I am forever grateful for the ways I've grown after burying my child, my parents, and now my sibling. There is no way I could be who I am today, or see the beauty I see, or feel the depth in my heart that I do, without those shattering losses and the truly agonizing days of grief that followed. Maybe it doesn't look like it, but I'm actually ten feet tall—and I'm not even one of the big guys out here in this beautiful world. I'm not exemplary in any way, this is just the grandeur of a mature human being. Adulthood could shine like wisdom, if we weren't afraid of growing out of our wounds and into ourselves. But even today, carrying the immensity that I do, I would never, ever choose to go through what I did to get here. This is why you have to go kicking and screaming to your fate at times.

These gifts are also not a sure thing. You can absolutely ignore the breaks in your heart, shoring them up with all the many options our culture doles out to numb the pain, or to wear your wound like an identity, crawling inside to live in stasis—these days it takes work to let ourselves fall to pieces. It takes courage to be undone, remade—but it's not a mystery. This is a pact we made with our humanness the day we joined the world: we find meaning and furtherance in adversity. To keep going we have to agree not to go numb, not to hide, shirk, blame, or deny. Transformation is painful. Being a person is messy. There's nowhere to go but through. These are the gifts no one wants. They are crucial and impossible, and what make us into people worth being. To receive them we must not remain the same, we have to let ourselves be affected, feel, be rightly heartbroken, and let that hot grief forge us into the giants we were made to be.

-Liz D. 1985

We entered this world on a turbulent wave of uncertainty and instability, bringing immense joy and hope to our parents.

People speak to us of the struggles of 2020, but all we know is love and togetherness. We don't cry much and we've slept 12 hours a night from our first month. The reason for this, we believe, is because we're always together. We're like grizzly cubs in a den, with tremendous love all around us. We're warm and fed, safe and stimulated, and have each other to play with and learn from.

And, even with all this isolation from the rest of the world, we've met many people this year. Although our trip to Indonesia was canceled this fall, we're still lucky to see our Great Grandma and Great Grandpa there, on WhatsApp, almost every day. We also get lots of cuddles from Papa, love to dance, play the piano daily, read and read and read, and enjoy licks from our big furry sisters, Pie and Cake. Their mouths might be dirty, but it's okay.

We want a world where love, faith, hope, kindness, peace, freedom, unity, respect, responsibility, and a healthy and sustainable environment triumphs.

WE LOVE LIFE!

-M&M S. 2020

A big impact on me this year was realizing the importance of human contact and interactions. I also have drawn on my faith more and more.

My dear husband was in a memory care facility with advanced dementia. As I tried to remain strong on my daily visits with him, I drew from these Bible verses. Psalm 31:24 "Be strong and take heart, all you who hope in the Lord." Psalm 46:1 "God is our refuge and strength, an ever-present help in trouble." Psalm 62:8 "Trust in him at all times, O people: pour out your hearts to him, for God is our Refuge."

In early March all visiting privileges with my husband were eliminated because of the COVID-19 quarantine. Toward the end of May, I got an urgent call saying he had contracted the virus and had a very short time to live. During the last 2 days of his life I was allowed to be with him in full protective gear. I thank the Lord for this special time together.

This year I've prayed and talked with God more frequently to give thanks for all the years my husband and I had together, for our family, friends, health, and countless other things. I also asked for guidance and strength to see me through these lonely difficult days. During this isolation, I realized the importance of human contact, whether by phone, Zoom, or social distancing, as we muddle through these difficult times.

-Marcia R. 1937

*T*he COVID-19 pandemic has affected me in different ways. First, the isolation that it has caused affects my freedom. I know it is important to wear masks, practice social distancing, and limit large group gatherings to help control the spread of the disease. Because of this, I have a greater sense of loneliness. I miss LaVonne deeply. The two of us would have been able to be there for one another and support each other. I also have a stronger awareness of the loneliness that my mother and mother-in-law have and are enduring.

My family has always been close and supportive of each other. Since Labor Day weekend 2014, we have gathered as a family at a resort. We range in age from seven months to eighty-four. The entire family mourned the loss of meeting but knew it was best that we postpone until 2021. LaVonne's family has grown closer as we have a greater sense of the health and well-being of the family members. We have cancelled holiday gatherings out of precaution for our safety.

I miss the church family also. We have not met as a congregation since March. Fortunately, the services are live streamed so I can attend that way. Sunday mornings were special to LaVonne and me as we attended church. The congregation is warm and cares deeply for each other.

-Mark Y. 1958

P andering politicians!

A nxious/ acknowledging blessings

N esting/Netflix

D eflecting/donating

E nnui/exercising/exasperation

M arginalized/ Micah 6:8/Matt. 25:40

I mpatient for justice

C ommit to action!

-Mary R. 1953

Living a life where I am medically more isolated than the average person, COVID didn't phase me. The increased isolation actually pushed me to get a new job where I could socialize with people. Although it is always necessary to protect ourselves and to stay safe and healthy, I believe it's also important to remember that none of us are guaranteed tomorrows. We need to celebrate each other and life while we're alive and able.

-Mary S. 1979

I have noticed that our family is of the utmost importance and my relationship with my husband is at the center, for sure. We have evenings with dinner and a good movie to relax and enjoy the time we had previously taken for granted. Both of our sons and their families call us on FaceTime each week, or more often, to check on us as well as share what is happening in their lives. Our grand children call often, too, as we do with them.

We have helped my brother and his wife move to Illinois to be nearer to one of their sons, and to be able to receive the additional care they need for macular degeneration and memory loss.

Outside garden work feels good and therapeutic, as does walking and reading.

We are thankful for what we have and all that we can do to help others.

Our new cars have added very few miles between mid January and late September, but they are safer for us to use during those few times each week.

-Mary Joy S. 1941

My reaction to the pandemic (as of January 2021) was one of surprise and great curiosity. Because I have a nursing background I watched with great interest all the details of the rising numbers of cases and deaths, discovering the virus, preparing to care for patients, changing the protocols of that care as more was learned, and producing and distributing the vaccine.

I have been appalled at the lack of cooperation with mitigation efforts, both from the federal government and from citizens of the U.S. Because of several health problems I have and my age (77), I have been extremely careful, essentially staying at home except to pick up groceries and doctor appointments. We have met with in-town relatives, but only outside with masks. I miss them very much. As I do work with the National Parenting Educators Network and Elders for Infants advocacy group I spend a lot of time on Zoom. So even though my physical world is small my Zoom world is huge! Although I am generally an optimistic person, I think the projects I am working on keep me motivated and happy, despite the horrors in the outside world. It does sadden me to think of the effects on the unemployed, communities of color and parents trying to work and school their children. It will take time to right our ship of state.

-Mary Kay S. 1943

My heart hollowed out from the loss of my loved one and living so many solitary moments caused by the virus. I have learned to savor the sweetness of times spent with persons whose soul I share.

-Mary Rita C. 1941

2020 was especially good to our little family of five. It allowed us uninterrupted time together like we have never experienced and probably won't again. Our jobs remained strong and our schools did an exceptional job of teaching our kids, first virtually and then back in the classroom. The experience taught us gratitude and humility; as we looked around we realized many were not as fortunate as us.

Like many crises in life, we are taught that if you aren't the ones suffering, you should quickly look for those that are, and help them. The pandemic did an extraordinary job of widening the gap between those who are suffering and those who are not. What we must remember is all of us will come across a time when we suffer; it is when we find ourselves with the most strength that we bend down and help someone else up. I hope our family has done that for others, it is something we strive for every day.

-Megan M. 1974 & Mike M. 1973

Spring, 2020, saw the convergence of the coronavirus, our 50th wedding anniversary and my wife suffering a stroke. Any one of these experiences would call for a reassessment; together, they challenged what I thought the future could mean.

Until recently, in my mind we were not old. Instead, the old were those who had gone before us, our elders. When I looked around more carefully, I realized we were the elders. It seemed both unfair and inescapable. Alarmed, when I asked my wife where the time had gone, she smiled and tapped the side of her head; it was all in our memory banks (museums?) if we were willing to look carefully and honestly.

Everything big and small seems to have become an adventure, and I find meaning in what I would have overlooked in the past. Not only have the adventures changed, so have the victories.

Maybe they should not even be thought of as victories. Rather, milestones or hallmarks or life lessons. They center on walking unimpeded outside, calling to mind old and new memories, telling family how much we appreciate them even if we are not together, reaching out to old friends across the years, letting go of others with dignity and compassion, and keeping foremost the Buddhist notions that being in the present is the only real answer to fear, and nothing in life is guaranteed beyond this breath.

-Michael M. 1946

Create More Than You Consume!

I've been committed to this—and especially now during the pandemic—by creating a stronger community here at the abbey, creating more flute music, and creating a stronger oblate community.

-Michael P. 1969

I WASN'T AROUND FOR WORLD WAR II. My benchmark for the Chinese adage *"May you live in interesting times"* was the Sixties. They were exciting, fun. I was much younger then. Although I don't feel or act (I'm told) much older now, I am a smidgen closer to wearing diapers... again.

The energy of the '60s–from Kennedy through Vietnam to Armstrong–along with my youthfulness back then led to optimism: We'll get through this!

Now I wonder. Am I walking too fast and is optimism splashing out of my bucket? There seems to be less. Or maybe it's cynicism that, I've heard, can sometimes creep in as one gains seniority.

The past four years have been annoying with our dysfunctional government and mentally unstable ringmaster. In this last year, things have actually become scary: The mismanaged pandemic, its economic devastation and bumbling of its vaccine distribution. George Floyd's lynching and related aftershocks. Most recently, a sitting president inciting an armed insurrection. The hits just keep on comin'.

I'm hopeful–not yet optimistic–that all of the current chaos subsides and is replaced by a new, inclusive "normal" that is peaceful and stable with great strides toward real racial and economic equality that rekindles widespread American optimism.

These are indeed interesting times.

-Mike M. 1948

I memorized the Boy Scout Law as a young teenager. Many words of the "Law" have often come to mind during the year 2020.

≫ Strive to be Trustworthy and Obedient to follow the rules that help reduce the spread of the virus.

≫ Strive to be Loyal and maintain family and friend relationships even though we are more isolated.

≫ Strive to be Helpful, Friendly, Courteous and Kind in interactions with people who may be the opposite of you in many ways and are most likely stressed during these times.

≫ A Cheerful and Brave (but safe) attitude can go a long way towards reducing anxiety during this troubled time.

≫ Cleaning your hands often is the new norm to help combat the spread of the virus.

≫ More prayers than ever are needed during this stressful time (Reverent).

-Mike S. 1951

*T*hings I've learned from the pandemic and beyond:

⚙ Our health is our best wealth.

⚙ To quote Robert Frost, "In three words I can sum up everything I've learned about life (with COVID-19): It goes on."

⚙ I learned from my 90 year old friend who survived the Holocaust, that being on "lock down" is a cake walk compared to living in fear of the Nazi's.

⚙ Wearing a mask in Minnesota cold weather keeps your face warm.

⚙ Wearing a mask makes our eyes "talk."

⚙ We're all separated together.

⚙ After months and months of no hugs, we realize all humans need human touch.

⚙ That our front line warriors continue to give and give of themselves day in and day out.

⚙ That technology has created some unbelievable moments for all of us.

⚙ The sun always comes up bringing with it hope for a vaccine.

⚙ Humans are survivors.

⚙ Always look up when things look down.

⚙ Look for the good in every day.

-Nancy R. 1943

The coronavirus demonstrated the mind-boggling, awe-inspiring, interconnectedness of our planet. It swept through without regard while unmasking social injustice. We masked and quarantined ourselves from the unseen COVID, we de-masked ourselves from the unconscious biases and structures that divide us. It was all messy and human, Jupiter and Saturn aligned for a moment, and the earth completed another rotation in the right direction.

-Nathan Y. 1976

These are trying times, with COVID-19, political partisan divide, and general depression and ennui from having to live in such restricted situations. We hesitate to socialize with those close to us, and we hesitate to discuss our political views for fear of heated arguments with those of opposing or at least differing viewpoints.

It would be quite easy to just give up on our country's future and on humankind as a whole. It would be easy to believe that things have never been this bad and will never be better. However, we must remember that we and our country and our species are all as resilient as we allow them to be. Our country has survived civil strife and even civil war. As a result, we have studied and sometimes applied what must be done to correct the situations that led to these. Humans have encountered devastating illnesses and suffered untold loss of life from them, but this has led to miraculous medical advances. Personally, nearly all of us have experienced traumatic physical and emotional events, but that has led to growth that we would not have had otherwise. In short, if we allow ourselves, we can develop scar tissue figuratively and literally that is stronger than the original it has replaced.

If we allow ourselves, we can survive and perhaps even thrive in the end.

-Otis L. 1949

COVID-19 CAUGHT ME OFF GUARD. A NATURAL WORST-CASE PLANNER, I WAS READY FOR FINANCIAL CRISIS, VIOLENT WEATHER, MY OWN DEMISE. NOW I ENTERTAIN MYSELF WITH THE ANSWER TO THIS QUESTION:

DO YOU WANT TO AMUSE GOD? WELL THEN, TELL HIM YOUR PLANS.

I DON'T HAVE THE BLESSING OF CLOSE RELATIVES—I'M A GENUINE ADULT ORPHAN. WHILE I AM NOT RECLUSIVE, I AM ACCUSTOMED TO LIVING A SINGLE LIFE. MY FRIENDS PROVIDE ENDURING COMPANIONSHIP. I AM HUMBLED WHEN I AM TREATED AS A FAMILY MEMBER AND IDENTIFIED THAT WAY TO OTHERS. COVID-19 HAS SHARPENED MY ATTENTION TO THESE CONNECTIONS IN MY LIFE. I HAVE COME TO REALIZE THEY ARE TRULY EXISTENTIAL TO MY HUMANITY, TO MY PHYSICAL AND MENTAL WELL-BEING—A TREASURE I MAY HAVE UNDERESTIMATED! THIS REALIZATION WILL FOREVERMORE INFLUENCE MY RELATIONSHIPS.

BESIDES COVID-19, CIVIC TRAGEDY AND POLITICAL UNREST IN MY COMMUNITY HAVE REEDUCATED ME THAT WE ALL POSSESS THE TOOLS TO HEED OUR BETTER ANGELS WHO DAILY SHOW US THE PATH OF GENEROSITY AND SELF-SACRIFICE FOR THE GREATER GOOD. IT IS TRUE THAT WE DO BETTER WHEN WE ALL DO BETTER! THE JOY OF BEING HELPFUL TO OTHERS IS A TERRIFIC ANTIDOTE TO ONE'S OWN FEAR AND INERTIA!

COVID-19 Y1 PROVIDED ABUNDANT TIME TO CONSIDER THE SPECTRUM OF CHALLENGES AMERICA FACES ON HER WAY TO "A MORE PERFECT UNION." NOW MY AMBITION IS TO RESIST DESPAIR, FORGIVE PAST MISTAKES, AND TO CONTRIBUTE WHERE I CAN. NEW MASK ANYONE?

-Paddy B. 1945

hen I was a little girl, my parents returned from a trip with a small gift for me. It was a pottery egg holder decorated with the words:

"Hope on… hope ever"

After almost eighty years, that phrase has always stayed with me and brings me joy.

Pope Francis announced he had a new word for tomorrow.

The word is:
Hope.

-Pat O. 1937

Our immediate response to the pandemic was to reach out to personal and professional communities to initiate a weekly "essential conversation" via Zoom, now in its 40th week. Our family has stayed in touch via electronic media adapting as best we can to stay connected. With a son in prison, we've had a constant reminder of how the cruel realities of C19 have affected our daily lives.

As both life and business partners, the pandemic has brought unprecedented opportunities to experience and share our deepest grief and despair with one another, along with sharing our love and opportunities with others each day on our Zoom calls.

With only one another to physically hug and have close-in, physical proximity, we turn to each other more. We are totally re-visioning our business of 26 years and are more willing to enter into conversations of depth and intimacy with our family, friends, and the greater community.

-Patricia N. 1953 & Craig N. 1946

"I'm so happy!"

These are my favorite words I like to say, because that's how I feel most of the time. Unlike many of my other verbal expressions, everybody can understand my happiness when they're around me. And that's part of why other people like being with me; including my special teachers, my family, and even people in the stores and out on the street who meet me.

This pandemic has not really affected me, except that I can spend more time with my dad, mom, and brother, and I get to FaceTime more with my Papa. They are always so good and loving to me, even when I can be a bit annoying (I especially need to give my brother a bit of space when he's not in a good mood, but that doesn't happen very often). Otherwise, I go about my days with my one-on-one teachers, riding on a favorite horse, using my iPad a lot, playing with my cars... and growing very fast!

If I had a wish, it would be that others could be as happy as me and that everybody could love their family as much as I love mine.

-Patrick S. 2008

During the pandemic, I miss our monthly game with a small group of friends, our weekly games with a 100-year-old dear friend (her living facility closed to visitors), traveling to our daughter and her family in Florida, and our weekly trips to the movie theater. Weekly phone calls to family and friends suffice, but do not equal the direct contact I have previously enjoyed.

Concerned about our safety, our adult son moved in with us mid-summer and remains a constant in our lives. Many other activities remain the same.

When I chose my career, I followed the best advice I received: "Choose a career you love and you will never work a day in your life." When I retired, several people emphasized having something to do that I love to occupy my time and that stimulates my mind. My days soon filled with the experiences; serving on non-profit boards and the care and maintenance of our home and property and other routines of everyday life.

My advice is to always have something you love to do. Take time to appreciate what you have. Enjoy those who are with you and those from whom you are apart in whatever ways you can. Celebrate your dear ones and re-invent the ways you show love to others.

-Paul H. 1942

Like in football, there are the

basics—or fundamentals—of blocking, running and tackling, I believe we'd all benefit from *concentrating on the fundamentals of faith, hope, and trust.*

Anecdotally, I have two friends that are very faithful guys. They are established in their careers and have been for quite a while. Both have struggled recently with panic attacks and very bad depression. And so, along with concentrating on the fundamentals, I'd also feel strongly that a note in your book may be:

Never give up hope.
Never!

-Paul K. 1958

We are extremely fortunate in that the pandemic did not have any measurable or even noticeable negative impact on us, beyond the extraordinarily shallow fact that our usual four major annual vacations were curtailed to just one significant trip. But even that had a silver lining in that the vacation was possible only because our children were able to attend school remotely due to the pandemic and we were able to celebrate Dia de los Muertos in person, a true bucket-list item for our family. In fact, while so many across the nation and world struggled immensely, both with the direct and indirect effects of the pandemic, our family was fortunate to be able to spend more time together, a rare commodity, as in normal times our schedules are filled with travel for business, events—be they social or work-related.

The greatest benefit of this pandemic has been the ability to spend nearly every minute together (both awake and asleep) for more than nine months and to emerge with our love for each other and for our children stronger than ever. We appreciate the terrible impact this year had on the lives of so many, and bemoan the fact that so many lives were needlessly lost or destroyed, but are grateful that our family has flourished during these dark days. We are now looking forward to a better 2021 for all!

-Paul S. 1975 & Deborah S. 1977

Even with so much fear, anxiety, sadness, grief, loss, anger, and chaos all around us during this tumultuous and extraordinary time, there is always reason to hope. I have depended upon the gifts of trust, letting go of my fear, and embracing gratitude for the blessings of life. The pendulum of life is fluid. This too shall pass.

Let nothing disturb you

Let nothing frighten you

All things pass away:

God never changes.

Patience obtains all things.

He who has God

Finds he lacks nothing.

God alone suffices.

– St. Teresa of Avila

Life is a beautiful blessing from God. Cherish every day. Today will never come again, so do something special. Be a blessing. Be a friend. Encourage someone. Take time to care. Let your words heal, not wound. Forgive. Be kind. Be gentle. Embrace hope. Show compassion. Be grateful and give the gift of your love most generously.

-Peggy O. 1966

Even more than the horrors of the pandemic—and they are legion—the murder of George Floyd and its aftermath have affected us profoundly. Visiting the site of the brutal killing brought home to us privileged, middle-class whites the reality of racial injustice as it exists blocks from our home and, of course, way beyond. If there's an upside to the George Floyd tragedy and countless other instances of racially charged deaths, it is this: Our nation has been forced to acknowledge the undeniable existence of systemic bigotry and—just maybe—begin to bridge the chasm that destructively separates THEM from **US**. From a professional standpoint, the pandemic has dealt an unprecedented blow to our conference and trade show business. For the first time in 44 years, we've had to cancel our annual face-to-face, in-person event. Instead, we'll be holding a virtual conference. Using online technology is versatile and satisfactory—but nowhere near as rewarding as being in person.

To end on a positive note, we're delighted by the outcome of the Presidential election and anticipate much better times ahead. America won't quickly recover from the "national nightmare" of the past four years, but it does feel as though a brighter, more hopeful day is dawning.

-Phil J. 1945 & Susan J. 1943

The year 2020 treated my family relatively well. Being retired, we had no income or job worries. With our children being adults, we did not worry about juggling work, home schooling, online courses etc. Despite the fact that for 10 months we limited travel, chose not to dine indoors with friends etc., we lived a relatively good life. My wife and I had ourselves, nature and we could connect via the internet. Rather than bemoan these small inconveniences we prayed for the less fortunate of which there were many. We were the fortunate minority. The year past brought to light for us our county's disparities in income, health care and work conditions. Time and enlightenment allowed us to put thoughts and words into action to help others. Through increased charitable contributions and giving of our time we hope to have helped others cope. These thoughts and actions on our part will not end with the waning of the virus. The questions I have as we move into 2021 are whether our divided nation can begin to come together and whether the political and social divisions will begin to narrow. Will a spirit awaken in us to become less focused on limited interests, and instead drive us all toward the good of America?

-Phil T. 1951

I'm a firm believer that things happen for a reason. Many times in my life I have asked the question:

"Why?"

or

"Why me?"

Only to find the answer in the form of a better solution, a brighter opportunity, a renewed possibility. Those were the times when I felt the powerful intervention of Our Divine Creator.

This year has been challenging and difficult for everyone. As a healthcare worker, I heard stories of personal, financial, emotional struggles from my patients, friends, relatives and co-workers. It was heartbreaking to hear about the deaths of people I was close to and not being able to visit them when they became sick, nor attend their funerals. But then I also heard stories of renewed family ties, of deeper bonding among friends and colleagues, of re-affirmation of one's faith, of genuine caring. I can't help but ask: "Is it you, Lord, talking to us? Did this pandemic happen to remind us to take a pause and think of what really is important in our lives?"

I feel blessed to be in a profession that serves and cares for others, however, it also equates to dedication, respect, commitment and trust. So I try to start my day with a humble prayer that I recite before my shift work, formerly as a nurse and now as a physician, asking for the Lord's blessing in all that I do.

-Ramona D. 1957

As Randy sees it: "We've been sheltering in place for 25 years!" We moved to the Black Hills of South Dakota that long ago, when we followed a vision that resettled us from city to forest living, from secure employment to a life of creativity, art and taking chances. So far, so good.

For us, 2020 was the loss of Janna's 94-year-old mother, who we were able to care for in home hospice, right at the start of the pandemic. We were lucky. We could hold her hand and say goodbye. Too many people didn't get that chance in 2020. By June 1 we were back in the Black Hills running our art gallery during a summer tourist season that surprised us both. It felt like the wild west. Along forest roads, people simply pulled over to camp, because the campgrounds were full. We saw holstered guns, confederate flags, and lots of red MAGA hats. Masks were politicized and half the visitors who came to our door turned away when they saw we required them; or they challenged our request and walked in anyway. Randy was polite about it. Janna tried to be. Randy was fighting to keep the arts and our business alive. Janna was angry at all the unnecessary loss.

It's winter now. The tourists are gone and the forest is quiet again. Local deniers remain, as thousands die each day. Mom visits the family in our dreams. Art and love endure.

-Randy B. 1958 & Janna E. 1960

On March 14th, we celebrated the retirement party of our friend and had planned a game night with six others for the 20th of March. Nobody at the party was wearing a face mask. In conversation, there was some concern about COVID-19 but everything was still functioning at a 'normal' level. That seems so long ago; little did we know the routine in our daily lives would change drastically. We never imagined the devastating consequences of the rising pandemic.

We have tried to adjust to all the changes. Spending more time at home, we put together several jigsaw puzzles and watched old movies that reflected better times in the country. We cleaned our closets and our garage and backyard and felt a sense of accomplishment. Life continues even though our political system is struggling.

We pray to God every day for good will and love for one another and for our country. We trust that we will succeed and will regain the self-respect and good standing of our country around the world. We pray for those who lost dear ones and for those who are suffering–for those with the disease, their caregivers, and their loved ones.

A lesson I take from this experience is to have patience with the inadequacies of this world and the fact that many are not coming to grips with those things that will save us.

-Rebecca H. 1945

When 9/11 happened, were we not all horrified? We worried about future terrorist attacks, new security measures were put in place at airports, changes were made that are now part of everyday life. How long did our personal resolutions last after that fateful day? Did we embrace the ideologies of being more thankful? Did we reach out to our friends and family more and tell them how much we really loved them? Did we have more empathy for people; did we pray more? Did we learn not to take our freedom for granted?

So now, during the pandemic, we ask: does human nature ever really change? Will all of our best intentions from our 2020 experiences endure? Or will they fade away as well; as time marches on and we return to everyday 'normal' living? How many times have I heard people say we are learning what is really important: dads and moms playing with their children is precious, families having dinner together the way it should be, simplifying. How could our society move so far from traditional family life that it has taken a pandemic to bring us back to center? How long will it last?

Is there a revelation about myself that has been revealed during this time? Was it painful? Eye opening? I can only challenge myself to embrace my humanity, strive to live a virtuous life, and persevere in my faith.

-Rena B. 1961

PANDEMIC. THAT DOESN'T SOUND LIKE IT COULD BE A GOOD THING. NOT ONE POSITIVE CAN COME FROM A PANDEMIC. LET ALONE A **GLOBAL PANDEMIC.**

AU CONTRAIRE, THERE ARE A FEW POSITIVES I'VE NOTICED:

PATIENCE. IN MAY TO JULY OF 2020, I'D WAGER WE'D BE OUTFITTED IN ELBOW PADS, KNEEPADS AND A HELMET WHILE VISITING LOCAL WAREHOUSE STORES AND NATIONAL RETAILERS SEARCHING FOR TOILET PAPER, WATER, AND HAND SANITIZER. BUT NOW, ON OUR REGULAR GROCERY SHOPPING DAYS—WE'LL PICK UP THOSE THINGS, IF THEY'RE SHELVED—EVEN WITHOUT THEM ON OUR SHOPPING LIST.

CORDIALITY. BEFORE THE VIRUS, WE'D BE GETTING OUR EXERCISE BY WALKING THE NEIGHBORHOOD. NOW, WE'RE MASKED-UP AND STILL WALKING. INITIALLY, THOUGH, COVID-WALKING WOULD BE HEAD DOWN, MAINTAIN YOUR PACE, LIMIT EYE CONTACT AND CONVERSATION. NOW WITH OUR COMFORT LEVEL, ITS HEADS UP, EYES WIDE AND AT THE READY FOR ANY NUMBER OF GESTURES OF ACKNOWLEDGEMENT FOR SUBURBAN HUMANS. MY USUAL—A SLIGHT TURN OF THE NECK FOLLOWED BY AN UPWARDS NOD (MY MAN-NOD). THIS MAY OR NOT INCLUDE SPEECH, BUT IS MOSTLY LIMITED TO "HEY," "MORNIN'," "AFTERNOO", AND "EVENIN'". ONLY DEAR ACQUAINTANCES ARE HONORED WITH A FEW SENTENCES OF REAL CONVERSATION.

FLEXIBILITY. THE ABOVE ARE PRIME EXAMPLES OF DEVELOPING FLEXIBILITY TO DEAL WITH THE OFT-CHANGING DEMAND OF THE VIRUS. REALLY PUTS THAT OLD SAYING OF MY PARENTS "YOU CAN'T TEACH AN OLD DOG NEW TRICKS" OUT TO PASTURE. I AM AN OLD DOG. RECENT NEW TRICKS LEARNED: ZOOM, MICROSOFT TEAMS, GOTOMEETING, AND WEBEX.

-Richard R. 1956

A pandemic is a harsh reminder of the importance of human relationships: the joy of family, the companionship of friends, the blessings of newfound love. We are, by our very nature, social beings. We need and yearn for interaction with others.

One of the challenging outcomes of the pandemic has been isolation. Aloneness can be painful; a crushing blow to the spirit. How can we find peace in the midst of turmoil and loneliness? For me, coping has been a three-step journey.

First, acceptance. Coming to grips with limitations on our freedom is not easy. The Serenity Prayer offers sage advice: learn to accept what cannot be changed. This has been a time for turning inward, digging deep, tapping the reservoir of inner strength. Second, listening with the ear of the heart. What is this experience teaching me about myself, about others, about life? And, third, faithfulness. How can I deepen my trust in God?

A verse from Psalm 46 sums this up for me and has been my constant companion throughout the pandemic: "Be still and know that I am God."

-Rob C. 1960

Looking back over 2020, we have coped with the pandemic and the fraught political environment much the same as many people; with concern, maintaining physical isolation, increased on-line video meetings with friends and family, and learning to be self motivated to exercise without going to the gym. We were moved by the 2020 poem from American author Kitty O'Meara, "And The People Stayed Home", which spoke to us and so many others.

The main lessons we have taken from this year are:

⇒ To continually remember how fortunate and privileged we and our immediate family are to have the resources to isolate and live in a comfortable environment with few concerns for our own physical needs.

⇒ To recognize how deeply embedded in history is our country's active placing of impediments to the success of many of our citizens, and our own benign neglect of the issues.

⇒ To accept the need to take a more active responsibility for the democratic processes of our government, at all levels, from local, through state and federal.

-Roberta B. 1956 & Bill W. 1957

"Boxes, pretty boxes made of ticky-tacky."

Some will remember that line from a song by Marvina Reynolds and made famous by Pete Seeger. Before the pandemic my life seemed more ordered, more predictable. I lived inside the illusion that I was at least somewhat in control, that elements of my life fit into neat, if not pretty, boxes and what fell outside the boxes God would sweep up to preserve my tidy image.

This COVID disease and all of its ugly tentacles continue to bless me with moments of clarity that pierce the illusion. Then it is my choice. Do I patch the pierced peephole and succumb to delusion, seeming to function just fine in the illusion, or do I open the aperture to see new possibilities, validating the vision of what can be, of what God can create in me?

-Ron J. 1949

We have lived a year of unexpected *grief* and GRACE.

The fragility of life and the illusion of control were laid bare. A shocking and dispiriting number of neighbors, friends, and family chose to embrace lies and conspiracy theories instead of science and the common good. We learned to live with minimal contact, a calendar emptied of the events that stitch our lives together, and the loss of people close to us whom we could not comfort or grieve.

Yet along with grieving all these things and more, we learned how to focus on the graces of a life constrained. Cooking and gardening marked the days, walks in the neighborhood replaced travel, and online chats reconnected us. We drew hope from the many who did act for others, providing food, shelter, health care, and other essentials. We learned to practice patience with those around us and within our own households. We unlearned the meaning of risk and perhaps for the first time, the value of quiet, measured days.

This is the time and place we have been given. We cannot control the unexpected grief that comes our way. But we can seek out the grace.

-Rose D. 1953 & Peter D. 1951

Six Lessons We Have Learned This Year:

1.We are in this world as brothers and sisters.

2. There is good reason why we call the earth Mother.

3. We are all living with this pandemic together.

4. The USA is more strong/fragile than we had thought.

5. God is ever more present and mysterious.

6. And through it all, with faith and hope, we are "walking each other home."

-Rose W. 1942 & Dick R. 1941

The pandemic has made me more distant from my family. As someone who lives in a different state and depends on being able to travel, I have not been able to see them much. However, I was able to foster much more meaningful relationships with my friends and roommates that live in close proximity to me.

Lots of my grief has selfish origins. Of the time I spend grieving, it is mainly about things that were taken from me. Once in a lifetime experiences such as studying abroad, a summer internship, senior year of college, my graduation ceremony and potentially my entry into the workforce—have all been altered due to this "new normal."

With all of that being said, those losses pale in comparison to what some other people have lost. My priorities have largely shifted towards identifying which friends I want to keep in close contact with after college—and money. The former because COVID-19 has taken away many of the group activities I used to do. However, of the people in those groups, surely I can't stay close to all of them. Identifying the "real ones" has been the name of the game.

Also, as someone about to enter the workforce, my financial security has become more present as I've gotten older. Significant blessings from the pandemic have been a full-time job offer and ridiculous amounts of time spent with my roommates I wouldn't have gotten otherwise.

-Sam E. 1999

I WILL CALL MYSELF GRATEFUL FOR GUARDRAILS.

Because of these guardrails, it has become easier for me to become who I am. I have found myself more thoughtful and considered about where I place value. My own set point for busyness is so much more clear to me.

Within these "guardrails" of the pandemic, my innermost and basic building blocks of who I am show up. Who knows what point I am on, on this line of my own evolution of self, but I do have a sense of having made progress while in this COVID-19 experience. Age sixty is a crossroads where I encounter these questions: "What is the best use of my time? Are my endeavors true to my innermost convictions and to what I value, and who I love?" Martin Luther wrote about limitations in *The Freedom of a Christian*. To me, what he says parallels how I have lived within the novel limitations of the virus. I have found a good equilbrium with my engagement in the world, and my inward, contemplative self.

My spouse, Mutty, says, "I don't let it bother me. I would like to go listen to some music, yeah. But I want to survive this. I want to survive this pandemic. If I don't survive it, well, then I can't tell about it with my friends in Jamaica; I want to tell my story about it."

-Sara T-D. 1960 & Mutty D. 1961

Despite the terrible toll the pandemic has had on so many, in a strange way this past year for me has been a gift, both personally and professionally. It has spurred me to step back from the busyness and distractions of work, news, and digital entertainment to refocus my attention on God. Spending time in silence and prayer has allowed me to slow down and listen for the gentle whisper of the Holy Spirit. Life is simpler now. I'm more thoughtful and intentional about who and what consumes my time and attention. I've learned to be more patient, calm, forgiving, loving, to listen more closely and to empathise rather than jump in and fix everyone else's problems.

I have found the words of Matthew 7:7 and the advice of the Spanish Carmelite mystic John of the Cross to **"Seek in reading and you will find in meditation; knock in prayer and it shall be opened in contemplation"** helpful as I try to discern God's will for me. Prayer has gifted me with a deeper inner peace that has strengthened and inspired me to find new ways to be and share love in the world. The words of a chant sung at a Carmelite church in London conveyed a simple message and profound wisdom about faith in God—"Trust, surrender, believe, receive". God's gifts are not always easily understood but are always good.

-Sarah G. 1964

2020

2020 has been disorienting–and strangely grounding. On one hand, the election, racial injustice, and COVID have led to persistent anxiety in me about the lack of moral leadership in our country, COVID-fog from non-stop Zoom calls, and confusion about safety during this pandemic.

Yet, what a gift, this disorientation! As it seems to be emboldening me to build a home office, learn online with people from across the globe, dream, march, challenge my beliefs, and listen to my heart. I own fewer clothes and have new signs in my yard. I'm astounded at how resilient my kids have been to new work and school routines, despite deflated dreams of new jobs, internships, commencement ceremonies, sports seasons, and study abroad. How they've matured, started new ventures, and how much I've learned about what's alive in them–and in me.

2020 has also revealed "The Weakness in Me"–like the Joan Armatrading song.

I've been having realizations of when I haven't spoken up, or not been an ally. It's almost too much to hold at times. It's hard to feel. No wonder people numb out with work, alcohol, the internet. It takes a lot of courage to be well, to engage, to speak.

Bigger forces are at work than we mortals control. We are no more immune to these forces today than any other generation. It is a humbling reminder. I hope I–and we–become better for it.

-Sherry E. 1965

THE YEAR 2020.

THE YEAR OF GREAT CHALLENGES.

THE PANDEMIC CREATES A TIME WARP FOR ME.

ON MY CALENDAR I CROSS OFF THE DAYS THAT HAVE PASSED BY

I LOOK AT MY STRATEGICALLY PLACED LARGE DIGITAL CLOCK NEARBY

SO THAT I CAN KEEP TRACK OF TIME.

MY COVID SILVER LININGS HAVE BEEN:

NEW FOUND TIME

SLOWING DOWN

TAKING TIME TO REFLECT

TIME TO CHOOSE HOW I WANT TO MAKE EACH A GOOD DAY

TIME TO CONNECT MORE WITH THOSE I VALUE.

MAKING A CONCERTED EFFORT TO CONNECT WITH STRANGERS—

    A TELEPHONE OPERATOR IN NEVADA

    A LONELY, TIRED CLERK AT MENARDS

    SOMEONE WHO SEEMS SO VERY DIFFERENT FROM ME

I STRIVE TO MAKE MY DAY ONE OF GRATITUDE AND ACCEPTANCE WHILE TRYING TO FOCUS ON WHAT IS IN ALL OUR HEARTS: GOODNESS, KINDNESS, COMPASSION. AND THE DEEP LOVE OF FAMILY, FRIENDS AND LIFE ITSELF.

-Sherry S. 1945

The wisdom I gained during the COVID-19 Pandemic could be summed up in one word:

PIVOT

Noun, the central point, pin, or shaft on which a mechanism turns or oscillates.

Verb, turn on, or as if on a pivot.

I am the noun, the point upon which the mechanism of my spouse and myself turns. And I am the verb, trying to keep daily challenges in balance and harmony by negotiating, with a sense of humor, all the sudden changes in life during this season of Pandemic.

My favorite quote, non-humorous, of this Pandemic is by Mary Shelley in her novel Frankenstein: **"Nothing is so painful to the human mind as a great and sudden change."**

In other wise words from the past:

"THIS TOO SHALL PASS."

-Shirley W. 1948

Declare a National Pandemic "encouraging" you to live with your partner 24/7, 365+, both together in the very same space. If that isn't a supreme test of partnership, I don't know what is.

Although we live in our own home, (a "cozy" one), it's nearly impossible not to run into each other multiple times every day. We have been married going on 38 years, and together as a couple for nearly 40—that's over half my life! It's hard to believe that one could be so fortunate.

One of my greatest joys is that even after 40 years together, I can still make her laugh. I love hearing her laughter. Also uniquely, I think, something will trigger a song title with both of us. Not only will we both think of the same title, but we will hear it in the same key!

Because of COVID restrictions, we have also spent more time together in the same rooms than any other time in all those 40 years. Yet we are happy to see each other every morning, and we still have our ritual sweet kiss goodnight "from above" (I'm sitting and she is standing, usually after watching a movie or TV show together), every night.

So I know for certain that not only have I found, but am happily living with my life's partner. Thanks, COVID.

-Steve B. 1948

During these past ten months I have prayed a lot about my role in the pandemic—what am I supposed to learn, how am I to be moved or affected by this?

I've learned my role is to help make change happen for all the parts around my life, family, prayer, social, recreational, whether or not to continue work.

As I'm just one of a few still reporting to work, I've had a role in making the changes necessary to keep our operations running smoothly. We have thousands of constituents that still need our services. I've had to develop the changes our staff works with and how we continue to deliver our services to constituents.

In my family, I've also had the role of enacting change to keep us safe, healthy, and sane.

The interesting revelation is seeing the needs of others.While serving them, I have been given great energy and life, with a sense of who I am and what I was made for.

-Steve B. 1960

In a word, 2020 has left us feeling terribly

e   x   p   o   s   e   d

Physically exposed to a life threatening illness that has taken the lives of friends, and could be lurking around the very next corner for us.

Morally exposed to the reality that we still haven't fully faced our own shortcomings on the subject of race.

Culturally exposed after seeing how far we've strayed as a country from common cause; wondering what it will take to re-weave our shared middle ground; wondering what our role in the healing should be.

Financially exposed when income and stability for some of our family and friends evaporated.

All this raw exposure is uncomfortable, and in some cases painful. It has challenged us to think more deeply, judge more slowly, appreciate our gifts more fully and recognize that we control a lot less in our lives than we'd like to think.

-Steve H. 1951 & Marsha H. 1957

At the beginning of the pandemic, the stay-at-home orders meant avoiding personal contact with others, including family. We have a blended family of six adult children and fourteen grandchildren, ranging in age from 12 to 26. Like all grandparents, we felt bereft and deprived.

However, we realize COVID-19 provided us with new blessings, albeit virtual ones. Feeling particularly lost at Thanksgiving, we arranged a zoom call with our family, who joined from California, Minnesota, Kentucky and Australia. In "ordinary" times, we are never all in one place. This year though, their beloved faces all popped up on the Zoom, and all interacted joyfully. We were all together in spirit.

In preparing for Christmas, we remembered our own good fortune and that of our family. We knew millions of others were suffering. We wanted to give our grandchildren more than presents... so we gave them the gift of charity. We asked each of the 14 to designate a charity to which we could donate in their names. We were proud how each thoughtfully embraced the challenge and shared the reasons for their choices. We learned of their big hearts and felt closer to each one. A virtual blessing!

-Susan F. 1946 & Dave D. 1934

HOW THE LIGHT COMES

I CANNOT TELL YOU HOW THE LIGHT COMES.

WHAT I KNOW IS THAT IT IS MORE ANCIENT THAN IMAGINING.

THAT IT TRAVELS ACROSS AN EXPANSE TO REACH US.

THAT IT LOVES SEARCHING OUT WHAT IS HIDDEN,

WHAT IS LOST, WHAT IS FORGOTTEN

OR IN PERIL OR IN PAIN.

THAT IT HAS A FONDNESS FOR THE BODY,

FOR FINDING ITS WAY TOWARD FLESH,

FOR TRACING THE EDGES OF FORM, FOR SHINING FORTH THROUGH THE EYE, THE HAND, THE HEART.

I CANNOT TELL YOU HOW THE LIGHT COMES,

BUT THAT IT DOES, THAT IT WILL.

THAT IT WORKS ITS WAY INTO THE DEEPEST DARK THAT ENFOLDS YOU, THOUGH IT MAY SEEM LONG AGES IN COMING OR ARRIVE IN A SHAPE YOU DID NOT FORESEE.

AND SO MAY WE ON THIS DAY TURN OURSELVES TOWARD IT,

MAY WE LIFT OUR FACES TO LET IT FIND US.

MAY WE BEND OUR BODIES TO FOLLOW THE ARC IT MAKES.

MAY WE OPEN AND OPEN MORE AND OPEN STILL

TO THE BLESSED LIGHT THAT COMES.

   -JAN RICHARDSON

-Susan S. 1936

I liken the pandemic to John Steinbeck's classic The Grapes of Wrath, and the migrants' journeys to escape their misery. They were hopeful, and many believed they were in God's hands, venturing out to a new life.

We are in that stage today, desiring a newness in many aspects of our lives... in the relationships with our children, with our church communities, with our extended families, and in our ways of believing.

At the same time, I grieve for those who have lost loved ones, including five that I have known personally. However, I'm also full of gratitude for many new friends developed during this tumultuous time, and my heart is full with the birth of new, dancing twin granddaughters, born in April, and the simple but beautiful send-off from a grandson: "Grandma, I'm going to miss you." Alas, the beauty and purity of young children.

We need to recognize the multiple gifts that are within our reach, and to help ourselves and others recover and move positively into 2021. Or, as Fred Rogers' mother said:

"To look for the helpers"

-Teresa R. 1954

"Life has no meaning. Each of us has meaning and we bring it to life. It is a waste to be asking the question when you are the answer."

-Joseph Campbell

*A*s I have aged, Campbell's words reflect my evolving convictions. Although he did not specify how we bring meaning to life, I automatically conclude that it comes from significant involvement with people. Living in this liminal time—a pandemic, a contentious political atmosphere, and social justice revolutions on multiple fronts—has had the effect of clarifying what is essential. When stuck in lockdown, I pine only for my people: cuddling up with grandchildren, helping my students, comforting my friends and family facing serious health conditions, freeing immigrants and people of color from cages or glass ceilings.

Admittedly, I searched for a Campbell quote. More authentically though, the verse that nearly daily echoes in my mind has a related theme. Micah 6:8 says, *"The Lord has told you what is good. He has told you what he wants from you: Do what is right to other people. Love being kind to others. And live humbly, trusting your God."* I have meaning because of the roles and responsibilities I embody in peoples' lives. Am I Love in the world? Am I Justice in the world? Do I take real action steps to foster a just world for all creatures?

Where lies life's meaning? As Campbell (and Micah) said, it is a waste to ask. **Just start being the answer.**

-Terrisa F. 1962

LIFE'S HARD.

But we can do hard.

-Tess C. 2005

My secret self-image is that of the

BULLET-PROOF DRAGON SLAYER.

You send the boogie men, and I will defeat them. I will slay them enthusiastically and with great panache.

After the scourge of pandemic and the relentlessness of 2020's constant curveballs I am still smiling and full of gratitude but my panache has petered some and more than a few bullets have broken through the armor, too many have been political.

I find time and spirit to rejoice in the one I love but realize that without my laughing and loving partner bleakness could have triumphed.

Perhaps it is being 71, or perhaps vulnerability has become painful and real, or perhaps I am not working hard enough to rediscover my enthusiasm. No matter the labels, 2020 and it's isolation has taken a toll.

BUT IT WON'T WIN.

Gratitude will win. Joy will win. Love will transcend. By the grace of God.

-Tim M. 1949

That moment is gone,
The one that was.
I didn't miss it,
but I didn't keep it either.
Even though it was familiar
There was nothing else like it.
Every splash in the same puddle
is like no other.
We are wise when we
look backward to learn.
We are fools when we
look backward to live.
I'll never see that moment
again.
But it will find me again.
Nothing is ever lost.
Not even time.

-Gary Ternes

-Tim T. 1965

I abruptly reached forward to turn off the news. There was silence, finally!

"Oh the noise, noise, noise, noise!" *

I had to disconnect. I'd heard enough!

What a year it's been. There seem to be no words to describe these tumultuous times. It seems we've been stripped of so much with COVID, terrible political divides, separations of family and friends, along with the challenges to our mental stability and common routines. There were fires, and other weather-related disasters, racial divisions, disproportionate poverty, and more, all impacting life further than I can ever remember.

Is there light at the end of this tunnel I ask? Can we get above the noise to a quieter more sane, peaceful place? I hope so. Does the gift of this Advent have particular meaning for us this year? It seems a perfect time for us to turn off, tune out, and look in new directions to refresh. Can "someday" begin now? How?

In this challenging time, can we be not afraid? What do we really fear?

Can we envision Peace, and believe we can find it?

Can we see new light or a different perspective, and understanding?

Can we rebuild trust and compromise, and really listen to one another?

Will we give into the possibilities of new ways of living for our future and the future for that of our children, grandchildren and our earth?

I believe we can build a better world together, because nothing is impossible with God!

*Dr Suess, How The Grinch Stole Christmas

-Tish O. 1939

As 2020 began, I faced a decision to take part in an experimental treatment protocol for a serious medical issue. I struggled with the many uncertainties involving this. Would I get an infection as the treatment increases this risk? Would it work? Would I suffer from one or more of the potentially-severe adverse effects? Should I not participate in the study and continue to monitor without treatment, the current recommended standard of care? As the coronavirus emerged and there were predictions of a deadly global pandemic, the uncertainties I faced multiplied and intertwined.

Now, after a year, I realize how much I relied on others for advice and support. My wife who has been a trusted and engaged partner throughout, my physician, trusted infectious disease experts, my employer, work colleagues, and my children all helped with decisions, adjusting my daily activities, and support.

Mentally, I was not managing this well, and I reached out to a therapist to help me cope effectively. I am halfway through the treatment protocol, no serious adverse effects, no Coronavirus infection, and the treatment is working very well. How did it work out that, so far, I seemed to have made the "right" decisions? Is it coincidence that this protocol became available just when I needed it, that I was presented with expert and trustworthy caregivers, and I had the strength to accept advice and ask for help without shame? Is Albert Einstein's quote "Coincidence is God's way of remaining anonymous" true?

-Todd N. 1956

The pandemic of 2020 has done things to me and for me on both ends of the spectrum. The first three months of the pandemic when everything was shut down was a fascinating time for me. I was taking a daily walk, eating healthy and praying in a different way. The first three months were like being on a sabbatical in a good way.

Then I began to receive messages from people in the community on how they were struggling with loneliness, mental illness, unhealthy households, etc. I realized how different the experience of COVID-19 has been for all of us. For some, like me, a time of reflection and quiet. For others a time of pain and brokenness. In the midst of it all I hope to be a person that represents hope and a reminder that Jesus journeys with us and is present in the beauty, but also the pain.

-Tom L. 1963

Like for so many others in the World, 2020 has delivered crisis, grief, and significant loss to our family. We have felt extreme versions of fear, love, anger, sadness, and hurt.

The gift of 2020 is that we learned life does not bring you meaning. You must find meaning in what life gives you each day, even in difficult times, **and the pathway to that meaning is love.**

-Tom W. 1963

Living in a dark place like prison during this pandemic, paranoid-epidemic-madness, has turned this place into hell. Even the administrative staff and officers came straight from hell to torment and treat us like crap. And on top of the pandemic, on outside of these razor wire fences, people are losing their lives for no reason only 'cause of their skin color. Pandemic is bad enough but the world is coming more to hate.

The twenty-three years of my time being in here, this year has been the hardest. I have almost lost control a few times. But then a dear friend and his wife reminded me of their prayers. I was becoming blind by **hate** for the administrative staff and officers and the happenings out there, but my friends and God set me back on the right track.

I looked up the meaning of wisdom. "Understanding what is true, right, or lasting" Good friends last forever, and God will never leave us. He is true and right and lasting for eternity, so without wisdom we don't have God, faith, common sense, belief, peace, love, joy, happiness. So I have wisdom, and I want more, like I want more of our Lord Jesus Christ.

This pandemic has learned me not to think it can't get worse, 'cause it can. So keep faith and give it all to our Lord Jesus Christ. And read, Ephesians 5:5, Philippians 3:13-14, Exodus 33;14

-Tony H. 1963

Reflection 1:

2020 is to be remembered as a Pandemic year. But what was the true pandemic? Illness? Vanity? Death? Hubris? Whiteness? Blackness? Political division and derision? While we may be living through a health pandemic, it is the politics of pandemonium that is without specific origin or vaccine that poses the greatest threat to humanity. Science can only save us from so much. The rest is up to our collective Human Spirit, and it is there we must place our hope.

Reflection 2:

How many "once in a lifetime" events can one generation live through? Are we really that unique, precious and fragile? Or have we decided challenging historical events are a threat to be feared, rather than evolutionary growing pains to be endured. How we deal with crises reflects the advancement of humanity and reassures us of the promise of Providence. It is comforting to reflect on just how resilient humankind has been over the arc of all history, even if we despair in the circumstances of our "present" history.

-Tony K. 1967

2020 was the most difficult year in my life. I lost my wife. We had been together for more than fifty years, and it is very difficult to talk about this experience now. Our family has not been affected by COVID; none of our relatives had it. This makes my wife's death, not related to this virus, even more tragic and unexpected.

My wife's passing-away made me think more about my spirituality; I became closer to church and will probably continue to explore that aspect of life. I am planning to move to Russia to join my son's family. This will be my third move to another country; possibly, the most difficult one.

My support is my family. It is good to realize that both my children came to me as soon as they could, and that we were together during the first several weeks after Tatiana's death. I will be a grandfather again in June 2021. It will be my fourth grandson; I also have two granddaughters. That I will be with my youngest three grandchildren (aged from 12 to newborn) in Russia gives me a lot of hope and sense to live and keep going. 2020 is a difficult and uncertain time; I hope that 2021 will be better. But I will always remember and mourn my wife.

-Valeriy S. 1950

I HAVE BEEN MOVING A LOT THROUGHOUT 2020. FROM ONE RENTAL PLACE TO ANOTHER (ALL BY CHOICE). THIS YEAR WE HAVE CHANGED FOUR LOCATIONS AND NOW HAVE SETTLED IN THE FIFTH ONE, ABOUT 100 MILES FROM MOSCOW. IT IS FAR MORE PROVINCIAL, QUIET, IN THE MIDDLE OF NOWHERE, LIKE BEING BACK TO THE USSR. HOWEVER, WE HAVE RUNNING WATER, ELECTRICITY AND A TOILET INSIDE THE HOUSE. THIS WILL BE THE FIRST TIME I SPEND WINTER IN THE RUSSIAN COUNTRYSIDE.

I HAVE BEEN GOING THROUGH AN IDENTITY CRISIS FOR SOME TIME NOW. LAST YEAR I WROTE A BOOK, BUT HAVE NO CONFIDENCE IN MYSELF AS A WRITER OR THAT ANYBODY WOULD WANT TO READ WHAT I HAVE TO SAY. I HAVE WRITER'S BLOCK, AND PROBABLY AM DEPRESSED, BUT I KEEP LOOKING FOR THINGS TO RE-START THAT ENGINE AND FIND THAT CREATIVE FIRE THAT I HAD TEN YEARS AGO.

I HAVE LOST MY MOTHER; IT IS DIFFICULT TO THINK ABOUT IT. PROBABLY, I HAVE NOT YET FULLY REALIZED WHAT IT MEANS TO ME. THIS UNDERSTANDING WILL PROBABLY COME, AND MY EXPECTATIONS TOWARD THIS HAPPENING ARE FULL OF FEAR.

MY WIFE AND I ARE EXPECTING OUR SECOND CHILD. WE WILL HAVE A BOY, WHICH MAKES US HAPPY AND FULL OF JOY. I AM LOOKING FORWARD TO HAVING MY FATHER LIVE WITH US AND SEE HOW HE PLAYS WITH GRANDCHILDREN AND PASSES TO THEM HIS KNOWLEDGE AND TALENTS. I AM MORE OF A REALIST THAN AN OPTIMIST, BUT I WANT TO BELIEVE THAT 2021 WILL BE BETTER.

-Victor S. 1977

We live in a senior community whose dining room is closed, exercise classes stopped, library shut, and programs forbidden. The pace of our lives has been throttled down, for the good of society we believe, but slowed, and some of the joy of community living squelched by the pandemic.

The pandemic also presented opportunities. Using a spiritual analogy, the year has been our "40 days in the desert"—time to reflect, heal, grow, and serve in unique ways. Some of the opportunities to which we were alerted and how we responded are: writing notes telling fellow community residents how valued they are; sitting with a resident's severely demented husband so the resident could get a mammogram, see the dentist, or buy some groceries; building a small snowman outside the window of a 95 year old shut-in—which thrilled her. (After a snowfall we'll build several snowmen around the building so many residents will be able to see them); learning the difference between the sheep and goats of Matthew 25 is that the sheep were alert to recognize opportunities to serve, and the goats were not.

The year brought some challenges. It also presented some unique opportunities. We are ready for our "40 days in the desert" to end but grateful for how we have been invited to live the year.

-Wayne H. 1935 & Marge H. 1935

Acknowledgments

"Gratitude" is a huge word, sometimes overused, but most often, a deep felt expression from the heart. It is this later emotion that has come over me as I read the final draft of 20/20 Wisdom.

To you, the 192 family and friends who gave of yourself for this book, please know that my heart is full of gratitude for your profound, inspirational, and challenging writings. Of course, this is YOUR BOOK, for it would not have happened without the giving of yourself to this project. Thank you a hundred times over!

For the second time in two years, Liz and Curtis brought their artistic and publishing knowledge and talents to the publication of the book, via North Star Press of St Cloud. Thank you both for creating such a physically beautiful book.

20/20 Wisdom would have taken much longer and been far less organized had it not been for the large number of hours given to it by my son Billy. His computer skills were a godsend, and his patience with me is to earn him a place in heaven.

Throughout the process, beginning in the fall of 2019, to its final publication, there have been numerous encouragers, affirmers, and candid auditors of the project. Among them go my thanks to Sherry E., John F., daughter Mary, Kevin L., my Monday Morning Faith Group, and numerous others, some of whom are not even in the book. You know who you are, and I'm indebted to you all.

When first considering this book, I turned to my wife, Teresa. With such a worldly and weighty subject, I was apprehensive as to whether I was up to the task. It was because of her enthusiastic and encouraging support that my decision to proceed was made. And she was there for me right up to this final writing. Without her this project would not have moved forward. Thank you my dear wife and partner!